IN THE KNOW

8 KEYS TO SUCCESSFUL LEARNING

Martin Good and Christopher South

BBC BOOKS

The material in this book is adapted from many
sources. The authors would like to thank those
concerned for permission to reproduce their
material; full details are given on p. 154. The
authors would also like to thank Suzanne Webber,
Senior Commissioning Editor at BBC Books, for her
ideas, encouragement and patience during the
writing and editorial stages.

Designer: Roger Daniels
Illustrator: Tony Garrett
Cartoonist: Glyn Goodwin

This book accompanies the BBC TV series *In the
Know*, first broadcast on BBC 1 from January 1988.
The series was produced by Julian Stenhouse and
Barry Tomalin.

Published to accompany a series of programmes
prepared in consultation with the Continuing
Education Advisory Council.

Published by BBC Books,
a division of BBC Enterprises Ltd,
Woodlands, 80 Wood Lane,
London W12 0TT

First published 1988
© Cambridge Training and Development 1988
ISBN 0 563 21367 1

Typeset in 10/12 Sabon by
Phoenix Photosetting, Chatham
Printed and bound in England
by Mackays of Chatham Ltd
Cover printed by Fletchers of Norwich

Contents

Introduction

In the Know puts you in the know about learning and gives you ideas on how to improve your learning skills, whatever the subject, from abseiling to algebra, book-keeping to boat-building, French cookery to French philosophy. The ideas can be used by anyone, from 16 to 60, and beyond, and apply to every sort of learning:

- for pleasure

- at work

- at college

- to improve your chances of getting a job

- so you can change jobs.

You could be learning informally or studying towards an exam or qualification. Either way the book will help you assess where you are now, and where you'd like to go with your learning.

If you'd like to extend the knowledge and skills you have acquired in this book there is an Open College course available, *The Effective Learner*, which is also written by Martin Good. This contains an open learning workbook and audio cassettes and goes into much more detail on many of the topics covered in this book. For further information write to: The Effective

Learner, Freepost, The Open College, PO Box 35, Abingdon OX14 3BR, or telephone the Hotline on 0235 555444.

How to use this book Each chapter begins with a summary and ends with a few pointers to what you may have found out.

The chapter has two types of text:

- the main text – which aims to inform and encourage you

- pencil and paper activities for you to try – which will help you think about and apply some of the ideas in the book.

You do not have to read *all* the information and do *all* the activities. Use it in the way that best suits you. You could:

- dip in (using the contents list) or skim through to see what catches your attention; then read the text and do some of the activities as you wish

- use it for reference – see if the book can help you with an aspect of learning that particularly interests you

- use it as a starting point – pick up the ideas and develop the activities to suit your own needs

- read the whole book – if that's what appeals to you.

Good luck with your learning!

1

Freedom to change

A perverse inability to fulfil our own potential is nothing new. It is something which has been worrying people for centuries. More than three hundred years ago, the poet Robert Herrick (who saw some changes in his own lifetime – starting out as an apprentice goldsmith and ending up as a clergyman) wrote a poem called 'Corinna's going a-Maying' which amounts to one long exhortation to avoid wasting our lives. Here are some lines from the final verse:

> We shall grow old apace, and die
> Before we know our liberty.
> Our life is short; and our days run
> As fast away as does the sun.

The lines seem as chillingly true now as they were in the seventeenth century. It remains true that we tend to see ourselves as trapped when in fact we are free.

We still fail to use our freedom to change our lives. We almost relish an opportunity to see ourselves as victims of fate.

A new start

It can take the shock of a calamity to open our eyes. A personal catastrophe like unemployment may release a dogged determination not to be left out of life. The redundant glazier spends his enforced idleness learning to be a juggler. It is a bizarre twist in his life and he may well go back to his old job. On the other hand, he may turn out to be a juggler of genius and never look back.

Personal myths

Do you have any of the attitudes below? Put a tick in one of the columns.

I think this way

	Often	Sometimes	Never
I won't change much as I get older.			✓
It doesn't make any difference how hard I try, I can't have much influence over what happens to me.		✓	
Feeling positive about myself is conceited.			
Thinking about what I want is selfish, I should always put others first.		✓	
I should put up with what I am not happy with – it is wrong to complain.		✓	
If I have problems it means I'm inadequate.			✓
It's better to keep my problems to myself.		✓	
It is undignified to have to 'promote' or 'sell' yourself.		✓	
I have no alternative to the way things are now.		✓	

Were some of your answers in the 'sometimes' or 'often' columns? If so, don't worry – identifying that these are negative attitudes is the first step to building up your confidence. Next time you hear yourself saying something similar (either just to yourself or to someone else) remind yourself of the positive alternative: for example, 'If I have problems it does NOT mean I'm inadequate.'

Stranger changes are happening every day. There is the story of the taxi driver who was in a crash which left her almost totally paralysed. All she had left was the power of speech. Struggling to come to terms with her terrible predicament, she had a curious thought. All her life she had harboured a secret ambition, but work, family and fear of looking ridiculous had held her back. Now, at rock bottom, she put an ad in her local paper:

She found her teacher and learned to yodel; she now makes money as a pub entertainer.

But you can make changes to what you do outside work as well. Perhaps that grey-suited clerk who looks so dull behind his desk is a fully qualified gliding instructor; the fees he earns as an instructor help pay

for him to go gliding alone. He finds his freedom in the clouds, but first he had to realise his freedom at ground level.

And the woman who presses clothes in a dry-cleaning shop eight hours a day goes home to her other identity as an accomplished wood-carver; she has been asked to make a lectern for her local church.

It would be insane to await a calamity to drive us into action. We must set our own pace and, with the guidance of good friends, steer our own course.

Do you know anyone who has significantly changed their life? Fill in *A change for the better* below.

A change for the better

Take a few moments to think about your friends and acquaintances – you are almost bound to come up with several people who have succeeded in altering their lives quite radically, either in their work or in their leisure.

Write down in the boxes what they have done and, if you can, what prompted them to make the change.

Who	What they did	Why they did it

Who's boss?

Let's look a little closer at that common stumbling-block: the conviction among wise sensible people that they are out of the race. Perhaps 'race' is not the perfect image for, although the world is undeniably fierce and fast, individuals are still in charge of their own pace. If running makes you miserable it is daft to go so fast. We can all crack the whip or tug the reins to regulate ourselves. And that could be your biggest discovery: you are your own boss and you are lucky to have such a good worker.

Today's beginner at any subject from oil painting to oil drilling has help available. An immense diversity of learning opportunities is available. But we still have to take the first step of acknowledging our own abilities.

There is an insistent voice in our heads that hates change because change is risk, and risk is a threat to safety, and safety is the whole purpose of the voice. This voice is tiresome, but it means well. Indeed, without that nagging voice mankind might well have blundered into oblivion thousands of years ago. Our taste for exploration and experiment would have been our doom. So we must not dismiss this Devil Who Says Don't. But we must not let him rule us, either. If he had his way, we'd still be living in caves with a life expectancy of about twenty-five. But we can expect a thorough negative nagging from that corner of our heads when we try to change things.

NO PROBLEM! Yas.

Meet a genius

To enter a new field of learning, however modest it may be, is to enter a state of change. The rewards will almost certainly exceed the effort, in self-esteem and self-knowledge if in no other way.

And self-esteem brings us back to that common stumbling-block. Our culture teaches us not to be vain, not to boast, but to strive for modesty. The trouble is, we carry modesty to extremes, parade our faults and hide our virtues. Most people have, at heart, a disproportionately poor view of their own inner resources. They have spent a lifetime making a close study of their failings but have neglected to look at

their powers. It is, for example, commonplace to find someone with a remarkable natural talent who cannot believe that that talent is not universal. It seems so easy that surely everyone must be able to see the moons of Jupiter with the naked eye, remember the entire Football League results at first hearing, ride a penny-farthing, and so on. If you tell these people they have a special aptitude they will probably scoff at your gullibility. Because the Devil in their heads has been lying to them, telling them they are dull.

If you want a chance to think about the skills you possess, look at *Clever you* below.

Clever you

Take a few minutes to make a list of all the things you are good at. Don't exclude any because you think they are mundane or commonplace. All skills are valuable.

Really; they are quite a lot.

You probably surprised yourself and came up with lots of skills. You may even have run out of space! Now don't forget that you have these abilities! They are an important part of you.

Early learning

Write down three things you remember learning during your childhood, plus anything you can remember about the way you did it. Examples are learning how to ride a bike, learning to swim, learning how to tie your shoe-laces.

What you learned   *How you did it*

1

2

3

Did you find it difficult? Read on.

We are all phenomenally good at learning. We are only in the foothills of understanding our own minds. When it comes to learning we cannot help being brilliant. We have all learned very difficult, complex things – how to walk and talk, for example. Information cascades into our skulls from the moment we are born and at an incredible pace.

Pause to consider the billions of facts you know about just a few brief years of your life: your childhood. Life seemed simple then, but your head was absorbing information at an incalculable speed.

Childhood learning

Can you remember how you learned things as a child? Look at *Early learning* opposite.

You may find it hard to remember your early learning. But you would be quite wrong to assume you have forgotten. It is all there in your head. What you may lack is the knack of getting the memory to the surface. There are a couple of reasons for the inability to summon up a memory from your early learning days, apart from the obvious one that in your innocence you simply did not register an event which seemed vitally important to the adults around you. It could be that you have such a mass of memories that your head is at a loss to know which one to recall. This is a problem of selection. It could also be that your powers of recall are suffering from a type of overload, or even that you are simply getting in a flap – you are so anxious to prove yourself by remembering something that your anxiety gets in the way.

If, after spending a while contemplating the mountain of memories you are storing from your childhood, you still need convincing that your head is amazing, then just think what has happened since those early days. Childhood memories are less than the tip of an iceberg. You have never stopped learning, remembering.

Word search

Think about what is happening at this very moment. You are reading a book – but is that all? Far from it.

Just to read this book your mind is submitting every word, every thought, to an intense scrutiny by comparing it with your previous experience. It is looking for patterns, it is trying to match these thoughts with other thoughts you have encountered in the past. You may become consciously aware of a few findings from this activity, but your brain will not bother to tell the conscious 'you' about all the possibilities it has eliminated.

For example, earlier we used the word 'glazier'. It is quite possible that the word triggered a search in your head for all sorts of significances in 'glazier', most of them irrelevant. You might know a pub called the 'Glazier's Arms', or you may have had a school friend called Sally Glazier, or you may be thinking about installing double glazing – any one of hundreds of associations with the one word.

Almost every word comes to us not naked and simple but trailing behind it and around it a swarm of special uses and senses. So to reply to the question 'What are you doing now?' with a simple 'Reading a book' is truthful but scarcely hints at the work your head is doing. But that work is very far from being the whole story. The complex process of reading represents only a fraction of what your mind is up to at this moment. It is, for example, ceaselessly scanning through a varying list of other possible activities to which you might wish to give higher priority. Is it more important to cut your toe-nails? Write a letter? Go to work? Go to bed? Listen to the radio? And there are scores more options. However hard you think you are concentrating, your head is in fact ranging far and wide, ceaselessly searching for other possibilities, only a few of which may be selected for conscious attention.

While this is going on, and your eyes are apparently glued to the page, your peripheral vision is keeping watch on what is going on around you. Any movement in the room will register instantly, even if you like to think you have cut yourself off from everything but the book.

Your other senses are all working hard, too. Your

ears are maintaining their own picture of your environment, checking every slightest sound against the vast archive of your aural experience to see if a buzz, click or hum has any useful significance. Your nose may not be as sensitive as a dog's but it, too, is scanning for clues to what's going on, checking for opportunity (the smell of a newly cooked cake) or danger (the smell of burning). Even your skin is vigilant, identifying any change in temperature or any discomfort.

All this and much, much more is happening while you simply sit and read a book. Everything happening to you now is being compared with your personal record of what has happened to you in the past.

Just how much experience we store may never be known. Yet we all know that phrase: 'I thought I'd forgotten until someone jogged my memory.' The lost fact was never actually forgotten, it merely evaded the search.

Mislaid information

You do not need to be particularly scatterbrained to set out from home to buy a certain object at a shop, but on the journey to the shop forget what it was you meant to buy. You have not, of course, really forgotten your errand. It might be more accurate to use the familiar phrase 'It's slipped my mind.' The information is in your head but 'mislaid'. What a lot of us do in this predicament is to retrace our steps, literally walking back into our own immediate past in search of the last conscious moment when we had the shopping list in the forefront of our minds. It is a strange phenomenon but we all do it. It can happen in the space of a few steps. We walk from one room to another, full of purpose, only to find ourselves standing in the second room with no recollection of why we are there. We have to go back to the first room and 'pick up the thread'.

These everyday and sometimes comical incidents clearly demonstrate one thing: we really forget very little. It is all there – if we can get at it.

Excuses, excuses

Because this process of learning continues without obvious effort we scarcely acknowledge it is happening. We who are naturally so adept at learning will readily deny we have any aptitude at all. We are not lying. We truly believe it.

If, instead of a blanket denial of ability, we declared: 'I'm not much good at book learning' or 'I'm hopeless at classroom learning', then we might be getting a little closer to the truth. For, although those sorts of learning and many other kinds may employ the same brainpower as our natural learning, they call for a significantly different approach.

We may need to learn how to learn. And we may as well face the fact that, while the vast majority of what we need to know to survive and lead our lives comes to us easily and informally, the tiny extra proportion needed to relaunch a life or open up a career can come hard to those of us unused to study. We may prove to be our own worst enemies. It is, for example, very easy to convince ourselves we are already too busy to tackle anything new. So manifold are our tasks and duties, we protest, that there is not a moment to spare.

Very often this is self-deception. There are very few of us who, by reorganisation and, if need be, ruthless elimination, cannot make time for something worthwhile. After all, we are talking about the way we spend the rest of our lives – who wants their epitaph to read: 'She was always too busy to do anything'?

When it comes to the pursuit of challenges, determination is vital. There has to be a degree of determination in anyone embarking on a course of study, whether for pleasure or profit or, with any luck, both. Almost any worthwhile activity means acquiring some sort of skill.

Even standing still and admiring the landscape takes time and effort. We have to train our eyes and our awareness to appreciate a view. The more we do it, the better we get. Unless we fight our natural tendencies to fuss over superficial matters, like wondering whether the bus home will be on time, the whole experience escapes us.

Fresh fields

We have discussed briefly how our memories accumulate millions of snippets of information as we pass through life and how, useful or useless, almost everything is stored for future reference. But why did such a mechanism arise in the first place? The answer is probably a very pragmatic one – it was vital for survival. Faced with a problem, our accumulated bank of knowledge and information can get us out of trouble. Of course we can amble along, wary of taking any risks with what our brain stores. We may well live to a ripe old age – and make very dull company for ourselves and our companions.

We have already mentioned the epitaph: 'She was always too busy to do anything.' How about 'He never took a chance' as an equally sad verdict?

Even the epitaphs 'She nearly made it' or 'He had a jolly good bash at it' are preferable to weary excuses.

Your epitaph

Ever thought about how you'd like to be remembered? Now's your chance to come up with your own epitaph! Write it down here:

Morbid? Maybe, but it may help you to remind yourself of what you want from life, and what you want to achieve. Learning could be a large part of that.

What Freud said

Sigmund Freud, the psychoanalyst, believed that we are motivated by two forces.

The first, called Eros (the Greek god of love), is a drive to get as much joy and pleasure as you can, with no thought of the future. All that's in your mind is the next packet of crisps, the next cuddle, the next game of snooker.

The second, called Thanatos (which is also Greek and means death lament), is a drive to submit to what Keats called 'easeful death' – a feeling that you can just lie down and go to sleep, accept the inevitability of the end.

According to Freud, the two are always conflicting forces in our lives.

Translated into learning terms, you can see this as the inner struggle between actively seeking to learn, and passively waiting for it to happen: taking control or being controlled. Take your pick!

And more excuses

Reasons why you should sit tight and do nothing will come thick and fast from various corners of your brain. A favourite line in excuses is: 'I had a bad start in life. I went to a bad school. My family were no help. It's not my fault. I'm a write-off as far as studying is concerned.' This is just one more attempt to shy away from change; self-protection at its most over-protective. The world changes all about you but your head's message is: 'Don't change. Change is chancy.'

Blaming an inadequate early education for shunning later opportunities seldom survives honest examination. Early academic excellence is not vital for later success. Yet we do try to prove to our own satisfaction that we are dull and incapable of learning.

Another trick often practised by the middle-aged is to drag up from memory some conspicuously clever classmate from long ago and use him or her as a hopelessly unattainable ideal. 'What's the use of striving when there are people as smart as Charlie around?' we ask ourselves, and cling for comfort to this thought because it lets us off the hook. We ignore any evidence that suggests academic cleverness is not directly related to achievement. Charlie may have been brilliant but where is he now? Working, perhaps, for a former classmate who never came top but had that certain spark Charlie lacked. Some of the most inventive and dynamic people in human history were poor scholars. But they went on to develop a power to learn that left the school prizewinners standing.

And at this point let us remind ourselves that the category 'late developer' is very real. It was not devised as a form of kindly condescension, a pat on the head for dunces. People change, just as the world changes round them. Our capacity to study may flourish awkwardly late in our schooldays or our lives, but we should not delude ourselves into thinking it is absent. It is there, waiting to be used.

Setting objectives

An early step in learning is making up your mind where you are heading. What do you want? What would it be sensible for you to aim at? You may be your own best judge here, but many people find it wise to consult a second opinion. After all, in approaching the prospect of learning to learn, your head has already put up quite a resistance.

Be precise when setting your sights. You may be

tempted to give yourself an easy ride or to saddle yourself with a back-breaking burden. Try to find out what your capacity is at the start of your studies. A good trick to play on yourself is to estimate in advance your own likely success in a test and then reward yourself when you prove accurate in your estimate. Do not give yourself a reward if you do better than you forecast. It may sound unfair, but it's one way to set sensible aims and find out exactly where you stand. So have clear aims set out. Be certain what you intend to achieve. Try to test your own ability. Get organised.

Try filling in *Setting objectives* opposite. It should help you use your particular strengths and avoid your particular weaknesses.

Guidelines

Here are ten useful guidelines to remember for successful objective-setting:

1 State your objective as precisely as possible.

2 Ask yourself whether there is an objective behind your objective. Ask why you want what you want – there may be other ways of getting it.

3 State clearly how you will know when your objective has been reached – this will ensure that your objective is clear and not vague.

4 State by when you want to achieve this and why.

5 Be clear that you want this for yourself, not for someone else.

6 Check whether any objectives conflict with each other.

7 Identify any *constraints* (external or internal) which will make your objective more difficult to achieve.

8 Identify any *resources* (external or internal) which will assist the achievement of your objective.

9 Check that your objective is realistic.

10 Ask whether there is anything to stop you achieving your objective now.

Setting objectives

Have a go at answering these five questions.

1   What do I really want to get from this course? Be as specific as possible.

2   What can I do to make sure this happens?

3   Based on past experience, what might I do to sabotage myself, and stop myself getting what I want?

4   How do I normally feel and behave if my expectations are not being met? Does this help me?

5   What can I do to maximise my chances of getting what I want?

Try to make use of your answers throughout your study – keep reminding yourself of 1 so you keep on target. Make sure you are carrying out 2 and 5 and avoiding 3. And if you are feeling the way you have identified in 4, ask yourself what has gone wrong with your studying.

What motivates you?

Write down an example of something you have done in the last week where your motivation has been

high

middling

pretty low

What does the word motivation mean to you? Use a dictionary if you like, but put down your own definition.

Motivation means:

Maslow's triangle The psychologist Maslow saw motivation as the desire to fulfil and satisfy what we as individuals see as our needs and wants. He categorised the levels of human motivation as

- body needs (food, warmth, etc.)
- security needs (to feel safe)
- social needs (to be a valued member of society)
- ego needs (self-esteem, other people's respect)
- self-fulfilment (to achieve one's potential, etc.).

Maslow saw these needs in terms of a hierarchy – the lowest needs at the bottom and the highest at the top.

The problem is that different kinds of needs may conflict. Your ego needs may take precedence over your social needs, or your self-fulfilment needs over your ego needs. You may very much want to improve your typing to 100 words a minute, but practising typing all evening may conflict with the desire to go to a disco.

Which needs motivate you in different situations? Fill in *Your needs* opposite, to see if Maslow's model applies to you.

Your needs

Write down five things which you recently wanted to achieve or do. Then in the second column write which need you were trying to fulfil, using Maslow's list.

What you wanted   *Which need*

1

2

3

4

5

The need to achieve In 1938 a psychologist called Henry A. Murray defined something he called the Need to Achieve, or nAch (pronounced ennatch). Here are the components:

- to accomplish something difficult
- to master, manipulate or organise physical objects, human beings or ideas
- to do this as readily and independently as possible
- to overcome obstacles and obtain a high standard
- to excel oneself
- to rival and surpass others
- to increase self-regard by the exercise of talent.

Some of these are about competing with other people; some are about competing with oneself, to achieve standards.

Murray went on to examine some of the characteristics of people who were high in nAch. Work through *The nAch quiz* overleaf if you want to assess yourself.

The nAch quiz

Answer the questions below by ticking your preference.

	greatly prefer	rather prefer	in between	rather prefer	greatly prefer	
1 I prefer being given work which I can be sure of doing well without too much difficulty.			✓			1 I prefer being given work that needs quite a lot of hard thinking to master.
2 I prefer having frequent opportunities to measure my own progress.	✓					2 I prefer doing tests rarely, not having to take a close interest in my results.
3 I prefer to work at my own pace.			✓			3 I prefer to work at the pace that is required of me.
4 I prefer to do work that can probably be done well.	✓					4 I prefer work that is difficult to do, but not so difficult that I would need luck to succeed.
5 On a course I prefer to be told early about the syllabus, the plan of working and what is expected of me.	✓					5 I prefer the person in charge to reveal the syllabus and the work, step by step, as we go through it.
6 I prefer to do work in which it is made clear just what to do and how to do it.	✓					6 I prefer work which requires my own initiative and judgement in deciding how best to do it.
7 I prefer to hear about an assignment immediately before I need to start work on it, and to know about only one assignment at a time.	✓				✓	7 I prefer to be told well in advance about an assignment, to plan when to do it, and to have several assignments to do at any one time.
8 I prefer to set my own targets and to have the chance to aim higher or lower when I see exactly how my work is going.	✓					8 I prefer to aim for targets which are worked out for the group and which are not chopped and changed according to level of ability or success with previous work.

Now you can score your own questionnaire. Each box on the table carries a different value:

	1	2	3	4	5	
1 work without too much difficulty	1	2	3	4	5	1 a lot of hard thinking to master
2 frequent opportunities to measure progress	5	4	3	2	1	2 rare tests
3 work at my own pace	5	4	3	2	1	3 work at a pace required of me by someone else
4 work that can probably be done well	1	2	3	4	5	4 difficult work but not so difficult it requires luck
5 told early about the syllabus	5	4	3	2	1	5 syllabus revealed step by step
6 made very clear what to do and how	1	2	3	4	5	6 requires my own initiative and judgement
7 learn about an assignment immediately before I do it	1	2	3	4	5	7 told well in advance about an assignment
8 set my own targets	5	4	3	2	1	8 targets set for me

For example, if your first three ticks were like this:

	this scores 1	✓				
	this scores 3			✓		
	this scores 4		✓			

You would score 8 for these three questions. You also score for each tick on the five questions that followed.

Put down your score for each question.

1 3
2 5
3 3
4 1
5 5
6 1
7 ....
8 5

Total score   28

Interpretation   Most people score between 12 and 32 on this quiz —
but whether your score is 'high' or 'low' is not import-
ant. However, it would be helpful to work on a course
that suits your style.

Score 31 or more — you will be happier working on a
course where you are very much your own boss. You
like to plan ahead to know where you are going and to
have a lot of independence.

Score 26 to 30 — you are rather above average in
your nAch when you study. You will probably be best
suited to courses that allow you considerable independence, but also give some guidelines within which to
work.

Score 20 to 25 — you are about average in your nAch
when you study. You will probably enjoy courses
which are fairly well organised, in which it is not
necessary to do much independent planning of your
own activities. Most teaching is designed for people
like yourself, or in the next group (15–19).

Score 15 to 19 — you are slightly below average in
nAch when you study. You will probably prefer
courses in which the students are told more or less
what is expected of them, there is little opportunity for
independent initiative, and the course of the work is
fairly closely controlled by the teacher. It may be that
your answers were related to a particular topic of
study that does not really interest you very much.
Most teaching is designed for people with your level of
interest.

Score below 15 — you are rather low on nAch when
you study. You prefer to do work where you can see
exactly what to do and can do it well, without difficulty. You may well find study rather dull; or at least
the topic that you were thinking about when you filled
in the quiz is dull.

There is no 'right' level for nAch. You may well have
a high nAch at work and low when you study, or high
on sports and leisure activities and low in class. Few
people have this trait in everything they do. Most
people have it in some things. The rest of this course
is about how to boost your own nAch — and hence
your performance when you study.

You should now
have an idea of how to
help build your
confidence
●
have a better sense of
your own abilities
●
realise the importance
of being your own boss
●
know how to set
objectives
●
understand more about
motivation.

2

Feedback

The simplest example of feedback is the information a baby gets when it puts its hand too near a flame. The baby was innocently exploring its surroundings. The fire hurt. This was the feedback. Now the baby knows more about the possible consequences of moving its hand. It has learned through feedback.

If you want to work out what the feedback is for other examples look at *Getting the message* opposite.

Feedback is essential. Without it your work will be lonely and unproductive. We have already discussed how each of us without conscious effort gathers a vast store of information from everyday existence. Now we will look a little more closely at how this happens, because we need to apply the same mechanism to our formal study.

Why we need other people

Put at its broadest, it is only through feedback that we know who we are and where we are. We could scarcely be aware of our own existence without feedback. We need a constant stream of information about how our actions or our presence impinge on the world.

Scientists have conducted many experiments to discover what happens when an individual is sealed away from such information. Volunteers wearing rubber suits, gloves, blindfolds and ear-plugs have been floated in tanks of blood-heat water with a backpack air supply to keep them alive. This sort of sensory deprivation quite soon had some very adverse effects on the volunteers' mental processes. They lost a sense of time and place and even began to lose their reason.

Getting the message

How do you get feedback when learning about these things? Fill in the 'Feedback' column. There may be more than one answer. (See overleaf for comments.)

Topic	Feedback
Hotness or coldness of water	
Strength of a rung on a ladder	
That someone likes you	
Attitude of a dog to releasing a bone	
How well you put up a shelf	

This shows how you can use feedback to minimise RISK. For example, you will RISK hurting yourself if you put all your weight on the weak rung of a ladder. You can avoid the RISK if you test the rung's strength first, by gently applying pressure.

Similarly, if you don't make learning feedback work for you, then you RISK not achieving your learning objectives.

Getting the message

Topic	Feedback
Hotness or coldness of water	Temperature on your skin
Strength of a rung on a ladder	Testing with pressure
That someone likes you	Smiles, body language
Attitude of a dog to releasing a bone	Growls and expression
How well you put up a shelf	Whether it falls down or not

Without feedback they were lost. One single thing could have rescued them from their unhappiness: contact with another human being. We value contact with others very highly.

Communication may come through books but even the most ingenious book cannot hope to be as responsive as a live human being. One thing is certain: without feedback we will not learn.

In learning, the need for human feedback, a teacher or mentor, generally becomes greater as the difficulty of the task increases. It is possible to learn to ride a bicycle by a process of trial and error – your feedback comes when you fall off. But the chances of learning to play the violin without a teacher are remote. In almost every imaginable case, learning is improved by sharing the study experience with someone else. Even threading a needle is easier if someone shows you how, or at least comments on your efforts.

Learning from our parents

In our earliest days, our parents are usually the greatest source of feedback. They can convey the lessons of their own experience through their response to our experiments. The child's whole notion of who and what it is, its mental picture of itself and its place in the world, comes to a large extent from the feedback of adults. The father stops his daughter's hand reaching the fire. So the feedback comes not from the fire but from the father. The child learns about fire, but not by the bitter experience of burning herself.

Too trusting

But the world plays tricks on us. We are continually having to reappraise our understanding of the way it works. Look at the example of riding a bike. Until we climbed on a bike we were probably convinced that the way to stop ourselves falling over is to resist any tendency to lean out of the vertical. But the opposite is the case when going round a corner on a bike. We have to learn to lean in a way that defies our earlier logic. Later, if we learn how to drive a car, we make the surprising discovery that when reversing we have to turn the steering wheel to the right in order to turn the car to the left. From clues like these we learn not to place too much trust in our own perceptions.

This is a valuable state of mind to achieve – one day that disconcerting moment will come when we learn that even our parents may be wrong. If we are to protect ourselves from the perversity of people and objects, we need to be more critical. We need to be the boss of our own little boat. The discovery of our parents' imperfection could be liberating.

As we grow older, the need to use our own judgement becomes more obvious. Our relations with other people grow more complicated. In the playground we learn how to choose our friends and how enemies are made, how to operate in a web of acquaintances, all of whom have their own perspectives on the world. We find out about ourselves by the effects our actions have on our playmates – their feedback.

In the classroom the teacher is the dominant source of feedback, the great mentor and monitor of our endeavours, and schools are often organised in a way which undervalues the pupils' judgement. Pupils are seldom encouraged to be their own bosses, take a hand in directing their own labours, yet they are held responsible if things go wrong, if they fail their exams, for example.

Be boss

If you now find yourself ill-prepared for formal learning it may not be entirely your fault. In Chapter 1 we discussed a tendency to blame ourselves disproportionately.

Blaming others can be just as futile.

But if, by trying to identify your own present shortcomings, you can chart your way to correcting them, this will be a constructive approach. If you feel you have been taught by rote by unperceptive teachers, then there may be no harm in saying so. But the discovery is useful only if you allow it to redeem things without bearing a grudge. Promise yourself that from now on you will strive never to let other people's inadequacies hamper your progress. You are the most important person in the learning transaction. The system is there to serve you, you are not there to serve the system.

Of course, unsatisfactory schooldays are not the only cause of a lack of expertise. To take an extreme case, illiteracy among people with perfectly good intellects is quite common and this can often be traced back to a prolonged childhood illness or a schooling disrupted by repeated household moves. For so many of us, our last day at school is a day of jubilation. It means escape from boredom and bondage. What a sad commentary on a decade or more of our lives.

In many cases the need for a systematic framework of study seems to have passed pupils by. We could spend a lifetime wondering why, but recriminations are a waste of time – it is better by far to try to sort things out for ourselves.

If you have left school and remember your time there as a bad experience, then try to approach a return to learning with a new spirit: you are now your own boss. If you are still at school and getting little or no satisfaction from learning, build on the advice given in this chapter: you *can* improve things.

Problem people

It would be unwise to assume you will get a lot of support from your present employer, if you have one.

Although there are increasing numbers of splendid exceptions, the most widespread attitude among employers to training or study is still a rather bloody-minded resentment when it comes to endorsing an employee's efforts. Many employers still prefer to poach a ready-trained worker rather than risk losing one they have trained themselves. For people in this trap, the only escape is to organise their own study.

Nor should you necessarily expect the wide-eyed admiration of friends. On the contrary, friends may criticise your absence from other activities or poke fun at your aspirations. Even families can be discouraging. You do not need to be a psychiatrist to rumble the mockers' motives. They may feel embarrassed or admonished by their own lack of enterprise. They may feel they are losing you to another loyalty – a modest educational aim can be described as 'pretentious' by people who have little respect for learning.

At these times, go back to basics. Remind yourself why you are doing it. Go no further until you have clear in your mind what you intend to achieve. If that vision fails you, then you have let other people undermine your confidence. Remind yourself who's boss. You are.

Supporters
Now, having discussed negative feedback from your problem people, let us turn to the people who can play an active role in your learning. You need their help.

We have considered the nature of feedback and its importance to anyone attempting to come to terms with the challenge of formal learning. But who is this vital element supposed to come from? There are a host of answers, but before we start scanning through your tutors, classroom colleagues, trusted friends and authorities within your community, do not forget to talk with yourself. This is not as silly as it may sound.

After all, you have known yourself a long time and you should value your own judgement. Set aside what you have been encouraged to think about yourself and go in for some tough self-examination. Are you being lazy? Overdoing it? Pretending you understand when you don't?

Self-questioning is all the more important if you are working on a course without a teacher or tutor. If so, try to find a friend to help you (p. 42) but, with or without that aid, practise assessing your own progress.

The package After yourself, the next most likely source of feedback may be the study package you have chosen. It will include its own commentary on your work, set tests, give guidance, focus your thoughts.

But it is other people – teachers, fellow students, friends, contacts – who are your best bet for feedback.

Your teacher If you have a teacher, take them first. When establishing a relationship with your teacher make sure your attitudes are correct at the outset. Remember the message: 'You are the boss.' When you were a child, the teacher was the boss. It was probably unthinkable for you to make demands. You got what you were given and that was that. You could not control feedback. If your schoolteacher's response to your work baffled you, left you with a feeling of resentment, failed to light a spark of enthusiasm in your mind, there was little you could do.

That was when you were younger. Things are different now. You have control over the responsiveness and usefulness of your teacher.

Want to know how to ask effective questions? Look at *Could you tell me – ?* opposite.

Could you tell me — ?

Read these three profiles:

A   is a manager aware that the boss is not satisfied with the way she communicates with clients on the telephone. He has told her repeatedly that she does not convey warmth.

B   is learning how to drive a car and, despite lots of practice, he is still finding it difficult to reverse accurately.

C   is studying for a book-keeping qualification. She has great difficulty in knowing how to start revising for the exam, and is re-reading all her books.

Put down a useful question each could ask the person teaching them, which would help overcome the problems they have.

A

B

C

Here are some possible questions:

A   Could you tell me two things you think I could say or do which would make me seem warmer on the telephone?

B   Could you tell me two things that would improve my performance at reversing, which I could practise specifically?

C   Could you tell me five questions I am very likely to get in the exam, and the best ways to prepare for those?

Now, can you say what points those questions all have in common? (See comments below.)

These things stand out:

- the questions are specific
- the answers can be measured in some way
- the person who asks the question has clear goals, and knows what s/he wants.

Did you come up with any others?

Bear these things in mind – they will help you to get the kind of feedback you need. Remember – your tutor may well have the factual information you need, but you are the expert on you.

Asking questions   The chart below gives a summary of things to remember when asking your teacher or mentor questions.

Why ask questions?
↳to find out opinions,
  information, facts

Types of questions
↦open questions   Use operative words: e.g.
  ↦to get background information   'WHAT do you mean by . . .'
  ↦to explore opinions   'WHERE have I gone wrong . . .'
  ↳to encourage discussion   'WHY is it better to . . .'
↦closed questions
  ↦to find out specific facts
  ↳to get YES/NO answers
↳probe questions
  ↳to find out in more depth

Questions to avoid
↦ambiguous questions
  ↳They confuse and mislead.
↦multiple/marathon questions
  ↳They also confuse and mislead.
↳rhetorical questions
  ↳They cannot be answered.

Preparation
↦Have clear objectives.
↳Have a list of questions ready.

Review
↦Really listen to the replies.
↦Check your interpretation is correct.
↳Make notes.

Tell me more   The best teachers thrive on being stretched by their students. They want their students to be demanding. They want to be pressed to justify their assertions and clarify their comments. If they are vague, they want to be asked to be precise. That way they offer their best

feedback and a truly potent learning situation is achieved.

That is the ideal. But we cannot guarantee ideal teachers. At worst, you may have a teacher with whom you have no rapport, who seems to have little grasp of your problems and who is disinclined to try. Your teacher's idea of feedback may be confined to a single word: 'good' or 'poor', both of which are almost useless.

You will be yearning to ask questions about what aspects of your work are being praised or criticised. Not in broad terms but precisely, specifically and in detail. You can scarcely make progress if you do not know where you have reached. This dilemma can be very frustrating if you are confident that your teacher is adept at the subject they are teaching. What a curse, for example, to be confronted with someone who is a brilliant singer but cannot pass on the know-how needed by someone with a good voice but no training.

It is happening all the time. It could happen to you. Is there a solution? If the problem is really what we call 'a clash of personalities' then check your own conduct to make sure you are not at least partly to blame, perhaps by appearing quarrelsome when you intended only to be questioning.

But if the problem springs from ineffective teaching, if the teacher is not explaining the subject in terms you understand and is not monitoring your work in a way that keeps you confident, then you really have only two courses of action: make the best of it or get out.

Getting out is almost never the better course. Instead, remind yourself of your aims and decide not to let anything get in your way. You may count yourself fortunate to have this learning opportunity at all. Make the best of it. Pump out of your teacher everything you can. Be demanding. Stand your ground. Insist on the feedback the teacher is there to give.

Just as we painted the blackest picture of family and friends opposing your plans, so we have painted the blackest picture of what you may find in the classroom. It could happen that way but it probably will not. Whatever happens, never cease to remind yourself that you are in control.

Fellow students   Still exploring the list of possible sources of valuable feedback, we come next to people with whom you may be sharing your studies. If you see yourselves as a team, or several smaller teams, you can greatly increase your learning potential. If you find among these colleagues one or more people who not only share the experience of the classroom but are also generally on your wavelength, then establish a bond with them. The old adage 'Two heads are better than one' is very true of learning.

If, for example, you can meet outside the classroom, get down to some serious discussion of your course content.

Although you have all been given the same information, you yourself may have picked up a vital thread that has escaped the others. They may equally well be able to fill a gap in your comprehension.

Taking notes in class is a special skill that eludes most of us. We end up with a systemless scribble. Part of the problem is that we are trying to do two things at once: take notes and understand what the teacher is saying or demonstrating. Try splitting this task between two of you. One concentrates on comprehending the shape of the lesson and the main burden of what the teacher is trying to put over. The other takes notes. The note-taker may miss out on the big picture but has a valuable list of references, headline reminders, detail and so on. Combine the two experiences and you will get a set of notes that will be invaluable in revision. What's more, preparing these notes as a team eases the whole task of learning.

If the two learners achieve a relationship of trust their out-of-class work together can be almost as valuable as what goes on in class. What's more, working with a group of fellow students is the most perfect example of feedback imaginable. The air between people at these times can be almost electric with shared respect and endeavour. Even the brightest student can find gaps in his or her comprehension which are easily filled by a friend.

That's what friends are for

Get the help of a friend – one who knows you well enough to grasp what you are up to and is patient enough to listen when you talk about it. One who will not only listen but respond. It is not important for this kind friend to know anything about the subject you are studying. But if he or she attends to what you have to say and then asks some sharp questions, you may find some unsuspected gaps in your knowledge. We all know that a fresh mind can work wonders. So find one. That's what friends are for. We tend to use the title 'mentor' for someone formally qualified to give guidance or teach, but anyone prepared to accept your trust and share your strivings deserves the title, too.

Is it going to be difficult to decide who to involve in your study? Look at *How easily do you take criticism?* opposite.

Giving criticism

You may get involved in helping someone else with their learning, which means you will have to give them criticism. When you do, consider these things:

- Have they heard it before?
- Is it a good time for them to hear it?
- Can they do something about it?
- State something positive.
- Express the desired result of your criticism.

If you find these hints useful for giving criticism, you could ask your own critics to try them out on you.

Clarification

One secret of using mentors, whether they are teachers or helpful friends, is not merely to ask questions but to offer them your version of what you understand your teacher has taught. Having absorbed part of the course, set out your version of it. This avoids perpetuating painful misunderstandings. The same goes if you are stumped. Spell out exactly what the snag is and insist on an equally exact clarification. Vague questions lead to vague answers and vague answers preserve ignorance.

A lively teacher will expect you to be lively, even

How easily do you take criticism?

Fill in the chart.

Can you take it?

People	Almost always	Sometimes	Almost never
Best friend			
Other friends			
Father			
Mother			
Brothers/sisters			
Colleagues			
Partner			
Any others? List them.			

This chart could be useful for deciding who to ask to be your mentor. It would be daft to ask someone whose criticism makes you feel antagonistic or defensive, or whose opinions you don't respect.

demanding, but this is an area in which we must each use our own judgement. The main thing to remember in establishing an effective relationship with a teacher is that whatever happens, you – the learner – must emerge from the experience better at your subject. A degree of diplomacy may be needed from each quarter but in post-school education you, the student, are the most important person in the classroom. In the last analysis, the only real test of a teacher's competence is the success of his or her students.

Jane, 42   *I had little knowledge of musical theory but decided I wanted to learn to play the jazz flute. I went to a teacher but we got along badly. He would make long statements, sentence after sentence without a pause. Here and there as he spoke I simply didn't grasp his meaning or was in two minds about what he meant. I was always in a state of indecision over whether to keep stopping his flow to seek clarification or to let him go on in the hope that the bits I didn't understand would turn out not to matter much anyway. That did not seem to me to be the proper frame of mind for learning the jazz flute, so I started to insist on having a chance, every now and then, to give him an account of what I had learned from his latest explanation. I couldn't think of any other easy way of making sure I wasn't missing something vital or galloping off with some complete misapprehension.*

But the teacher found this increasingly tiresome. Maybe I was being too demanding, but I certainly wasn't being combative for the sake of it. I was the client and I desperately wanted to learn. He was the teacher and I really think he did very much want me to learn. But having prepared his lesson, he did not like its logical progress to be disrupted by me, the ever-doubting student!

If only I'd had some idea which bits really mattered and which bits were only general background information it would have been some help. But what I really wanted was to hear his feedback on my account of what I had learned from him. This would have kept the whole course on the rails instead of what happened – we both rather lost heart and gave up.

Who was most to blame for this sad outcome? Was the teacher being bloody-minded? Was the student being a pest? The questions are very difficult to answer. Perhaps the teacher should have been much more receptive to the learner's demands. After all, he was the student's servant in a sense. Perhaps the student should have been less overtly demanding. True, the student was her own boss and there would have been no point in letting her lessons drift by in a fog of misunderstandings. Students should undoubtedly be demanding. But bringing a teacher to heel is not the object of enrolling as a student. The aim is to learn the subject.

If learning a subject involves using a little old-fashioned tact along the way, then so be it.

One final word on this tricky topic. How much energy should a student put into pleasing the teacher? The only sensible answer is: just enough to show the teacher you are neither dull nor mediocre but have a spark that will see you through. There is no purpose in shining in the classroom with your ready smile at the teacher's quips, your quick questions and eager enthusiasm if all this disguises yawning gaps in your understanding. It is not difficult to fool a teacher into thinking you know more than you do. But what's the point? What's wanted is a good working relationship which both teacher and student find rewarding. When all's said and done, the only person you really *must* please is yourself. You set your own sights and you are in charge.

Contacts Finally, use your contacts. Most people do not think of themselves as having 'contacts' in the way a businessperson or journalist has. But your community will probably have at least one person already proficient in the subject you are studying.

Say you are studying radio technology. The local butcher may be a 'radio ham' with a good knowledge of the basic principles of wireless telegraphy. Talk to him. He will get as much out of it as you.

Horticulture? Lace-making? Computer programming? Rack your brains, find a local expert. Everyone likes to be consulted, so they are most unlikely to rebuff your approach.

Your learning personality

One of the important factors which affects the way you learn and study is your personality – the kind of person you are. For example, some people are happy to work all day in the silence of a library; others prefer to study and talk at the same time, so they like being in a room full of people. Some will be willing to ask questions at a lecture; others are unwilling to risk making a fool of themselves.

Check out your personality with this list of items (which are based on some standard tests, but are more light-hearted). There are no right or wrong answers.

Look at the two sets of statements; if you feel one of them is very true for you, tick the box nearest to it. If it is fairly true, tick the next one along. If you feel you fall between the two extremes, tick the box in the middle.

1 Cool — Warm

Cool	1	2	3	4	5	Warm
Keep your problems to yourself	✗				✗	Get involved with others' problems
Keen judge of character				✗		See the best in people
Cool and methodical					✗	Tend to confide your problems
Tend to withdraw when things go wrong	✗		✗			Perhaps a bit muddled

2 Concrete thinking — Analytical

Concrete thinking	1	2	3	4	5	Analytical
Don't enjoy puzzles		✗				Like puzzles
Think slowly through logical problems	✗					Think quickly through logical problems
Prefer to think in concrete terms				✗		Often think in abstract terms
Tend to rely on instinct in complex situations			✗			Analyse complex situations in depth

3 Excitable — Calm

Excitable	1	2	3	4	5	Calm
Readily show feelings when upset				✗		Keep feelings hidden
Easily get angry			✗			Always stay calm
Open and emotional						Level-headed and unemotional
Fight for the right thing						Get the right thing through diplomacy

4 Accommodating — Assertive

Accommodating	1	2	3	4	5	Assertive
Tend to go along with others						Tend to insist on rights
Tend to put up with unpleasant things						Tend to object to unpleasant things
Enjoy easy-going groups						Enjoy critical groups which discuss problems openly
Tend to accept the will of others						Tend to take the lead

5 Quiet						Talkative
Quiet and cautious						Bubbling and enthusiastic
Rather reflective						Very active – not very reflective
Discreet and rarely outspoken						Frank and outspoken
Sober and concerned						Talkative, perhaps even a bit thoughtless

6 Expedient						Conscientious
Tend to be a bit frivolous and casual						Tend to be responsible and careful
Tend to disregard rules and regulations						Follow rules and stand by obligations
Easily change plans, even give up						Tend to persist, even if it's hopeless
Happy-go-lucky						Strong sense of duty

7 Shy						Venturesome
Uneasy with new acquaintances						At ease with new acquaintances
Socially retiring and sensitive						Socially bold – fairly thick-skinned
Reluctant to intervene						Willing to intervene

8 Tough						Sensitive
Hard, even a bit too hard at times						Gentle; sometimes need sympathy
Tough, perhaps a bit cynical						Kindly, a bit soft
Practical and logical						Sensitive and intuitive
Keep to the point						Thoughts and words may wander at times

9 Trusting						Cautious
Unsuspecting						Somewhat mistrustful
Overlook others' mistakes						Resent others' mistakes
Undemanding						Hard to please, suspicious
Flexible						Inflexible

Your learning personality (continued)

10 Down-to-earth						Preoccupied
Conventional and alert						Unconventional
Earnest but steady						Enthusiastic but apt to give up suddenly
Usually concerned with immediate things						Often lost in thought; a bit other-worldly

11 Natural						Shrewd
Spontaneous and natural						Polished and subtle
Contented and a bit artless						Ambitious; with an exact mind
Genuine, if a bit clumsy						Socially aware; self-conscious
Sometimes naïve and simple						Worldly-wise and shrewd

12 Unworried						Prone to guilt
Confident; a bit uncaring						Careful; a bit anxious
Unworried by disapproval						Worried by disapproval
Vigorous; rarely feel guilty						Apt to be slowed down by feelings of guilt
Always cheerful; a bit insensitive						Sometimes off-colour; brooding

13 Traditional						Experimenting
Conform						Inclined to rebel
Accept traditional values						Often question traditional values
Prefer well tried ideas						Tend to prefer new ideas
Keep to trusted methods						Experiment with new methods

14 Participative						Independent
Often a joiner						Often a loner
Rely largely on team work						Rely largely on own initiative
Sociable and group minded						Rather self-sufficient
Tend to agree with group's point of view						Often disagree with the group

15 Uncertain							Precise
Don't care for social niceties							Observe social niceties
A bit tactless and untidy							Controlled and sensible
Follow own urges, sometimes unwisely							Reliable and predictable
A bit unreliable; wild and woolly							Think ahead; rather right and proper

16 Easy-going							Keyed-up
Relaxed; sometimes a bit too serene							Keyed-up and rather tense
Composed							Often agitated
Calm; a bit unresponsive							Responsive; a bit irritable
Sometimes a bit dull							Sometimes rather fretful

Interpretation

These comments are about the way each personality factor could affect the way you study and learn. When you are thinking about taking up some form of study, bear them in mind. You may want to try to change and develop in ways that will make it easier for you.

1 Cool	Warm
Enjoy solitary study	Like to work in groups
Probably enjoy studying things	May prefer to study people

2 Concrete thinking	Analytical
Need time to think	Enjoy discussion
Prefer simply written, well illustrated text	Happy with indigestible textbooks
Work slowly	Like analytical topics
Like to use memory	

3 Excitable	Calm
Perhaps tend to be distracted easily	Like to settle and get deeply involved
Enjoy inspiration	

4 Accommodating	Assertive
Accept others' point of view – maybe a bit too readily	May tend to dominate discussions
May not like to enter into discussion	Readily enter discussions

5 Quiet	Talkative
Not keen to talk to people	Enjoy talking to people
May get over-serious	Generally light-hearted

6 Expedient	Conscientious
May prefer work to be handed out on a plate and may avoid difficult challenges	May find it hard to break out of habits of thought

Your learning personality (continued)

7 *Shy*	*Venturesome*
Not happy in group discussions	Happy with discussions
Find it hard to ask questions in class	Like project work
Prefer solitary work	
Need tactful and encouraging teacher	
8 *Tough*	*Sensitive*
Prefer others to be tough;	Like tasks involving imagination;
may be a bit intolerant	may like arts and music
9 *Trusting*	*Cautious*
Like working with others	Not happy in groups
10 *Down-to-earth*	*Preoccupied*
Like topics where attention to detail is important	Like to use creativity and imagination
11 *Natural*	*Shrewd*
May prefer practical subjects to abstract ones	May prefer more abstract subjects like law or sociology
12 *Unworried*	*Prone to guilt*
Happy to work under pressure	Better with continuous assessment
Not put off by exams or tests	
13 *Traditional*	*Experimenting*
Prefer traditional teaching methods	Happy to try new approaches
Teacher-led, highly structured	Happy to take more responsibility for learning
14 *Participative*	*Independent*
Not happy in competitive environment	Happy to compete and work alone
15 *Uncertain*	*Precise*
Prefer strong teaching	Like to know why the various activities are suggested
Like a lot of structure	Like things to be rational and clear
May have trouble writing good essays	
Notes may tend to be too long	Very good at taking brief concise notes
16 *Easy-going*	*Keyed up*
May not be demanding of self	May overdo things
or rigorous in subjects where that matters – eg computer programming	May demand too much of too little time
May not finish all the homework or push self to the limit	May get upset when things go badly or get difficult.

You should now
know why feedback is
important

●

have ideas on how to
develop your feedback
skills

●

be clearer about who to
ask to be your mentor

●

know about your
learning personality.

This chapter is about

how to organise your
time

•

how to set priorities

•

aids to organisation.

•

developing your own
system

Getting organised

How good are you at organising yourself? Have a look at *How organised are you?* opposite.

Order out of chaos

When we come to making order out of chaos, some very mistaken notions exist. For example, being tidy is often equated with being organised. Untidiness, or what looks exactly like untidiness to an outside observer, can be an acceptable or valuable part of an organised system. In some cases tidiness can even be a bad influence. Yet we find untidiness widely denounced as a sin.

The trouble lies in how we define the word 'tidy'. If we mean putting things in rows, whether or not the most often used items are closest to hand, then tidiness may not be the best arrangement. However, if by 'tidy' we mean arranging things in a logical way which works for the person using it, then tidiness is highly desirable.

How organised are you?

For each question put a tick by the most appropriate answer.

1   How much do you plan your time on average?

Not at all   A bit   Quite a lot   Always

2   Do you use a diary to plan?

Not at all   A bit   Quite a lot   Always

3   If you are learning, do you organise sessions for practice or private study?

Not at all   Occasionally   If possible   Always

4   Do you make and keep organised notes?

Not at all   A bit   Quite a lot   Always

5   Do you put things away when you have finished using them?

Not at all   A bit   Quite a lot   Always

6   Do you have close by what you need for studying?

Not at all   Occasionally   Often   Always

Using the answers to those questions, can you say whether you regard yourself as

very organised   average   not organised

Now read on . . .

Your time

Tick the column which seems closest to your answer to each question.

		Often	Sometimes	Rarely
1	Do you write daily to-do lists?	✓		✓
2	Do you prioritise your to-do lists?			✓
3	Do you finish all the items on your to-do lists?		✓	✓
4	Do you think you deal effectively with interruptions?		✓	✓
5	Do you allow yourself quiet time for working every day?	✓		
6	Do you allow yourself some free time every day?	✓	✓	
7	Do you put things off until the last minute?	✓		
8	Do you focus on preventing problems before they arise rather than solving them after they happen?	✓		
9	Do you meet deadlines with time to spare?		✓	

Orderly systems   The key question is: does it work? What you must find is a durable, orderly system which works and which is not so elaborate that it dominates your work or becomes impossible to maintain. If you achieve this and someone then tells you your system is untidy, take no notice!

You are responsible for creating your own orderly system. The classroom or workplace, the teacher or tutor, the teaching equipment – they will all be useless if you don't.

Time management

One of the most important things to organise is your time. How well do you think you are managing at the moment? Look at *Your time* (above) to find out.

	Often	Sometimes	Rarely
10 Are you on time to classes, to work, to meetings and to events?		✓	
11 When you are interrupted, can you return to your work without losing momentum?		✓	
12 Do you do something every day that moves you closer to your long-term goals?	✓		
13 Can you relax during your free time without worrying about work?			✓
14 Do people know the best time to reach you?	✓		
15 Do you do your most important work during your peak energy hours?		✓	
16 Do you begin and finish things on time?		✓	

Give yourself 4 points for every Often you ticked, 2 points for every Sometimes, and 0 points for every Rarely.
   Add up your score and compare it with the scale below:

Your time scoring

45 – 64 You seem to manage your time very well. Are you happy with things the way they are? Do you organise your time this way by choice? Do you think you are flexible enough?

33 – 44 You manage your time well some of the time. Perhaps you could try using your time management strategies more, and have a go at some of the ones in this chapter.

21 – 32 You could benefit from better time management – try out ideas from this chapter to see if you find them useful.

 0 – 20 OK, so your time management is not too good at the moment, but don't panic, and certainly don't despair! This chapter is here to help you. Try out as many of the suggestions as you can – you could be surprised by the results.

Dividing up your time   Most of us rarely analyse our time and divide it up into things like 'school', 'job', 'leisure', 'sleep', and so on. But it can be useful for seeing what we use our time for, and whether we want to make any changes. Try *Time-share* below.

Time-share

Divide your time up roughly into categories, e.g.:

- your job (if you have one)
- school or college (if you go to one)
- housework
- study or homework
- sport
- free time.

These categories may not suit you, so come up with ones that do. Put them in the first column of the chart below. Then put down approximately how much time you spend on each category every week.

Category

Hours a week

Surprised? Is there anything you would like to change? What would you like to spend more or less time on? Are there some things which you are not in a position to change?

Timetables   Now you have analysed your time, think about using a study timetable. It may help you to

- establish a target at which to aim

- spread your study over the week

- get down to things, instead of having to decide what to do next.

How about something like this?

	7–9 a.m.	9 a.m.–3 p.m.	3–5 p.m.	5–8 p.m.	8–11 p.m.
MON					
TUES					
WED					
THU					
FRI					
SAT					
SUN					

Have a go at one of your own – see *Your timetable* below.

Your timetable

Design a timetable for your own use and arrange the time segments to suit the pattern of your day. You may want to divide the weekend up differently from the weekdays.

Fill the chart out for the week ahead, but don't be over-keen and fill every hour with study. Once you have filled it in try to stick to it if you can. But don't worry too much if you have to alter things – be flexible.

Experience and common sense establish your proper pace. Your first plan will very probably be wrong. Rectifying error is almost a definition of the whole learning process.

Progress report You could also use a chart to monitor your progress, giving yourself grades for quality of work and effort, and to set down any action you need to take as a result.

Quality of work

A   Much better understanding than before.

B   More confident; generally better understanding.

C   Problems seem to arise just as frequently.

D   I'm having trouble keeping up.

E   I'm completely lost.

Effort

1   Working very hard.

2   Working harder than planned.

3   Sticking to my plan of work.

4   Not taking quite enough time or trouble.

5   I need to start working now.

The chart could look something like this:

Date	Subject/course	Quality	Effort	Action needed

Self-interruptions Are you one of those people who gets interrupted during your work? A person's average uninterrupted time at work is less than ten minutes! Imagine how much you could do if you had large blocks of uninterrupted time. Look at *Am I interrupting myself?*

Take a break

Some people really do demand a monastic cell, but many more can discover surprising powers of concen-

Am I interrupting myself?

Try this short questionnaire. It is not meant to be a serious test. Your answers will probably depend on how you feel or what you are doing at that moment. Put a tick in either column.

		Yes	No
1	Do you extend your coffee or lunch breaks?		
2	Do you procrastinate?		
3	During the day, do you use chat to avoid getting down to things?		
4	Do you read tempting material when you should be working?		
5	Does your mind wander throughout the day?		

It's not necessarily bad to answer 'yes' to all questions. But you may find it useful to think about your choices in these situations. You can choose to use your time like this, or you can choose not to.

tration in the face of many distractions. Those distractions can even be quite useful. For example, prolonged periods of reading can be less effective than a series of shorter bursts. The need to nip downstairs to make sure the dinner isn't burning in the oven can be a godsend. It could be good for your state of mind to take a brief break.

You may find yourself repeatedly wandering away from your place of study to go to the toilet. If you do, you may also accuse yourself of laziness or time-wasting. Do not be so swift to condemn. The need to stand up and walk about may seem silly, but it is probably quite sensible.

You may feel the need to slot back into the 'outside world' for a moment, and why not? Near the centre of the university city of Cambridge is a very large area of public open space called Parker's Piece. There are houses, offices and colleges at its edges but nothing interrupts the acres of turf except a single ornate cast-iron lamp standard in the middle. Walking across Parker's Piece can be a strange experience – so much space in the middle of a busy city. Perhaps that is why some joker has scribbled a two-word message on the lamp standard: 'Reality checkpoint'. The joker was probably a student who saw some parallel between long periods of study and walking across a huge empty area of turf. In studying, you may need a 'reality checkpoint', even if it is something as simple as going to the toilet.

The sort of organisation you will be creating for yourself will not be regimented. But it must incorporate a plan. There should be nothing rigid or inflexible about this plan of yours. What it really is is a clear statement of intention. It declares: 'I intend to do this, this and this and I intend to do them in this sequence and at this pace.' But it also says: 'If I find sticking to this plan has become unconstructive, ill-advised or just plain silly, then I'll look for ways to change it.' After all, a straight line is not always the quickest or best way between two points. The great test of a route is whether you arrive at your intended destination in a sensible way after a reasonable interval, without having made yourself unnecessarily miserable on the way.

How to plan

A lot of us tend to jump straight into doing a task as soon as we know what it is. But we are missing out several steps in between – steps which make up PLANNING, the skill of thinking ahead and deciding action. Have a look at the diagram below.

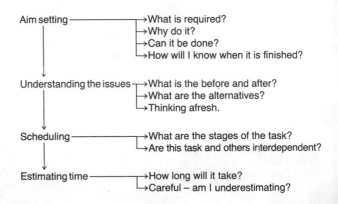

Aim setting
→ What is required?
→ Why do it?
→ Can it be done?
→ How will I know when it is finished?

Understanding the issues
→ What is the before and after?
→ What are the alternatives?
→ Thinking afresh.

Scheduling
→ What are the stages of the task?
→ Are this task and others interdependent?

Estimating time
→ How long will it take?
→ Careful – am I underestimating?

Try this out on a task of your own, even something mundane like washing your car.

Did you find it useful?

Remember – allow time for planning, but not so much time that you never get down to action.

Where to study

An early decision to make is where you can study on your own. This can be quite a problem. Even as a child tackling your first homework you may have found it hard to get away from the hurly-burly of family life for an hour or so. It can be worse as you grow older because you have more responsibilities and other people may be making more demands on you. We will be coming to the tricky topic of family relations a little later, but one hint on the choice of a workplace is: don't be too fussy. Don't make assumptions about what the ideal study spot is.

The conventional image of an ideal place for reading and writing is an absolutely quiet room, free from all interruption. That type of situation suits some people down to the ground. But many other people are put off by such total detachment from the world. You may find you need the noise of your family or your community in the background. If you accept the 'perfect silence' image without questioning that it is best, you might be needlessly anxious about your failure to find this wonderfully quiet spot. You might even become unreasonably tetchy with people who spoil your precious peace. Examine your true needs. They vary greatly from individual to individual.

Background noise If you examine your real needs honestly, you could discover that you prefer studying against a background of noise. Many surgeons have discovered that background music helps them concentrate in the operating theatre.

What is more, the human power to cut out unwelcome noise is quite remarkable. We have the knack of screening sounds and deciding which ones to bring to our conscious attention. You may have noticed how an irritating noise had failed to irritate you until someone drew your attention to it. Until then, your head had been sparing you the pain!

Storing your materials

When setting up your workplace, one item will probably be essential: a cupboard, shelf or drawer in which you can store all your work materials, your books, files and so on. If these materials are allowed to drift around the home or if they have constantly to be carried from place to place it will hamper your studies. Too much time will be spent merely setting yourself up for a study session. True, finding a place for your materials may be difficult if you are studying a subject which requires a great deal of hardware apart from books and papers. But do try to solve the problem; it will be well worth it.

One side-effect of an arrangement like this is that each time you return to your study place you will slip more easily into the most helpful mood for work – the abstract 'shape' of your work and your place in it will come back to you easily because of the physical arrangements you have made. An office often has this effect on people who work in one.

Don't delay

Now, one word of warning on this whole business of setting yourself up with a place to study and the equipment for it. We are all very adept at kidding ourselves, and one way we do this is by devoting ourselves to nest-building so we can put off hatching eggs. In other words, we enthusiastically apply ourselves to perfecting our workplace and getting the ideal work materials, when our underlying motive is delay. Don't be fooled – there is no substitute for simply getting down to it. And it could be unwise to invest in costly equipment until you are sure what your course requires. Fancy equipment in itself can be a delusion. Four-colour ballpoint pens which change from red to blue to green to black at the touch of a button are very clever but pretty well useless for most practical purposes.

Remember, in solving all these questions of working pattern, working place and working materials you have been blessed with judgement: use it!

The power to organise

You are gifted with a natural power to organise your life: use it in your normal learning.

And do not doubt you possess this ability. Just as in Chapter 1 we demonstrated your phenomenal natural ability to learn, so we must now show you that you have a similar ability to organise. Consider how the world hurls at you an endless stream of information which has no value at all unless it is organised. A relatively humdrum activity, such as crossing a busy street on foot, entails making organised sense from billions of observations. Most of the information coming into your head has no practical relevance to reaching the other side: the colour of the clothes of people on the far pavement, whether there is an aeroplane in the sky overhead. These and millions more are examined and set aside. By a process of winnowing or sieving, your mind, partly as an act of will, partly as an unbidden process of great rapidity, works out the moment to step off the pavement, the path to follow and the pact to keep. Almost every moment of every day is an endless succession of organising and deciding so that you survive. Your most trivial act is a miracle of organisation.

Anyone who organises a coach trip to the seaside tends to be hailed as a 'born organiser' but this sort of organising is trivial compared with the sort of brilliant organising going on unheralded in your 'disorganised' head.

Keep an open mind

An obsession with tidiness can be a very bleak approach to life. Tidiness can be a sign of a closed mind. Once everything has been put in order, the tidy person's duties are done. Nothing new is attempted – there is no creativity in such a scheme. Meanwhile, an apparently untidy person whose desk looks a mess may well have a clear enough understanding of where everything is.

This is not to recommend untidiness to the tidy. Simply stay the way you are. If you prefer to operate in superficial muddle and it works for you, then do not expend energy trying to mend your ways.

The people who say 'I'm no good at organising' are often the people who in Chapter 1 were saying: 'I'm no good at learning.'

The trouble is, it is even harder to convince them of their error if, on a day-to-day basis, their lives really are muddled.

But the muddle is probably not a sign of incapacity to organise. It is much more likely to be a symptom of a lack of enthusiasm. It can be desperately hard to do well at something we detest or for which there is no hope of reward. So if people who are embarking on a course of learning find themselves losing heart because they think they will not be able to plan their work, then they are almost certainly mistaken. They lack not the power but the spirit. Things will be different now that they have set their hand to something they deeply desire to do. They already have the power to organise themselves: now they feel the need to tap that power.

Priorities

To start thinking about priorities, have a go at *Ten things I want to do in my life* opposite.

Urgency and importance

It can be quite easy to confuse urgency and importance; separating the two in your mind may well help you with priorities.

Urgency – must it be done now, or soon, or can it wait?

Importance – what will you (or someone else) gain by doing it?

For example, buying a birthday present for a friend whose birthday is in two months' time is probably quite important, but not at all urgent. Whereas filling your car up with petrol because it is about to run out is both very urgent and very important. Can you think of things which are important but not urgent? These will probably be your long-term aims, such as spending more time with family or friends.

Ten things I want to do in my life

List ten things in the first column. They can be anything at all: from becoming a parent to meeting the Queen. In the second column list how important each one is to you – give a score of 1 to the most important, and a score of 10 to the least important.

Importance

1

2

3

4

5

6

7

8

9

10

Did you learn anything new from this? Where does your learning come out in importance?

If the activity surprised you in any way, summarise what it was and how it will affect your plans and priorities.

To see how you can use these definitions for working out your priorities, have a go at *Priority grid* overleaf.

Priority grid

Take nine things that you have to (or want to) do. Include a few long-term aims. List the nine things:

1

2

3

4

5

6

7

8

9

Now look at the grid below and put the nine things in the boxes. The most important and urgent things will go in box 1A; the least important and urgent in box 3C. Important long-term goals will go in 1C.

		Urgency		
		A (Do now)	B (Do soon)	C (Can wait)
Importance	1 High			
	2 Medium			
	3 Low			

The idea is to do things in 1A first – they are the highest priorities. Then tackle 1B and 1C, then 2A and so on. Don't be tempted to start with the things in 3B and 3C just because they are easy and undemanding – they are also not important, or urgent.

Did you find this useful? Maybe you could fill out a grid like this for the tasks in your learning, such as reading particular chapters in books, going to the library, talking to your teacher or tutor, checking your own progress in the course.

Bear in mind that your grid will never be static; the contents will always be changing, with new items being added. So your 1Cs will probably be 1As by the time you do them.

One last point: don't spend a whole day working out your grid. Find a compromise between thinking time and doing time.

A few tips Here are some ideas for how to deal with high importance activities:

1   Build your day around high importance activities;
    schedule less important items for the time left over.

2   Stay focused. Put distractions aside and keep the end
    results in mind.

3   Set deadlines. Make them specific.

4   Divide projects into smaller units. 'By the inch, it's a
    cinch.'

5   Get help. Sometimes you can't do it alone.

6   Use your peak times. Attack difficult things when you
    are mentally sharpest.

7   Reward yourself. Keep yourself motivated.

8   Make a commitment. Full speed ahead!

    And here's how to deal with low importance activities:

1   Ask someone else to do them to free your time.

2   Trade them with someone else – swap chores.

3   Systematise them. Use check lists and get a good filing
    system.

4   Lower your standards. What is the minimum accept-
    able level of quality with which you can get by?

5   Ignore them. Some things are better left undone
    (reading junk mail, etc.).

6   Pay someone else to do them (if you can afford it). Eat
    in a restaurant or hire a housekeeper.

7   Group them together and do them all at a set time.

The four 'D's If you have a mountain of things to do the four 'D's provide you with another way of getting organised:

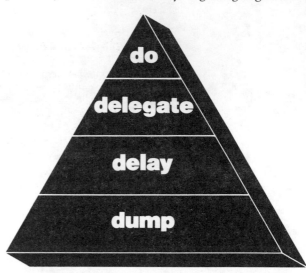

Start at the bottom and climb your way up the mountain. DUMP anything that does not really need to be done at all. DELAY what you can't dump. DELEGATE what you can't delay – get someone else to do it for you. And if nobody else can do it – or if they refuse – you'll have to DO it!

Advice on priorities

What advice would you give to this person? Use the priority grid idea if you think it helps.

A wants to be a financial administrator and is working to pass her examinations. She is not so much interested in the exams as in being competent. So she has set herself the task of reading the whole of six books, some of them about finance law, and is enrolling right, left and centre for seminars on all sorts of topics relevant to her job. (See comments opposite.)

Your advice on priorities:

Free-wheeling

Simply allowing your mind to free-wheel over a problem of organisation can do the trick. It is reassuring

Advice on priorities

Compare your advice with these thoughts:
A reasonable set of priorities would be
1   to pass the exams
2   then to build up wider expertise.
Passing the exams will give her the chance to spend even more time learning other things. But to pass, she needs to focus on the things that will get her through.

how the head can sort out a tangle almost without our conscious intervention. If we learn how to use this ability, we will see how all the jumbled pieces of a problem can be put into a sensible sequence.

Sometimes we really knew the solution from the start but our anxiety hid it from view. So we should never underestimate our innate powers of organisation.

Be flexible

Don't sit back and let your head switch on to auto-pilot. You need the flexible plan of action described earlier, keeping your progress constantly subject to review, making modifications in the light of experience. If you are studying, say, the history of aviation and halfway through the course television begins showing a good documentary series on the subject, on the very evenings you have set aside for reading, then it would be self-defeating to miss the programmes in order to read the books. Can you find another slot for your reading? Or, if you can tape the programmes, adapt your plan to accommodate viewing time. Either way, changes are called for and it is not a sign of weakness or vacillation to adjust your route if you are still on target.

But do make that target feasible. Be your own boss, but not your own tyrant. If you set yourself so great a challenge that you run a high risk of failure, you could end up weakening your confidence.

Be equipped

Card indexes

Equip yourself with the tools of your new trade. A card index, for example. We have said your head is a good organiser, but the best of performers can need a

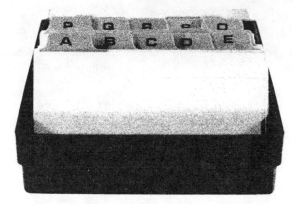

prompter and prompting is one purpose of an index. It can provide quick recall of information which might otherwise take you ages to retrieve. If, for example, you are studying forestry, it might be handy to have a card devoted to lime trees which would merely remind you of a few key facts and give page references in your textbooks. The very act of updating your lime trees index card would remind you of previous entries and fix the latest entry in your memory. Whether you run the index on a simple alphabetical basis or form subject groupings within the alphabet (so that 'lime trees' would appear before 'mulberries' in a subsection devoted to types of trees, with other subsections devoted to, say, the diseases of trees) is up to you. But if you make your index too elaborate it could become more of a millstone than a tool. Keep it simple. Effectively organised, your index can be a very valuable revision resource.

But bear in mind that when setting up a card index at the start of a course, you can scarcely expect to know in advance what demands will be placed on it in the weeks ahead. It should have flexibility built in. If you were studying, for example, journalism and on Day One of your studies you established a card index system based on your preconceptions of the subject you might confine the index to such categories as 'Use of Language', 'Gathering Facts' and 'Organisation of the Media'. This might work well enough at first, but you would soon regret that you had not started special categories for, say, 'Law' or 'Technology'. If you had already begun to enter technology references under 'Organisation of the Media', you could well end up in a muddle. The worst that can happen is that you try to force your course to fit your misconceived index. Keep it simple, flexible. That way it can be bent to changing needs.

Diaries Keep a diary to chart your path ahead and also to record what you have done. Entries in the diary need not be works of literary merit. What is needed is simply a record of work done and work to be done, together, perhaps, with notes on your developing team association with fellow students. You may be surprised to discover how reassuring your diary can be. There will be times when you will feel all at sea in your

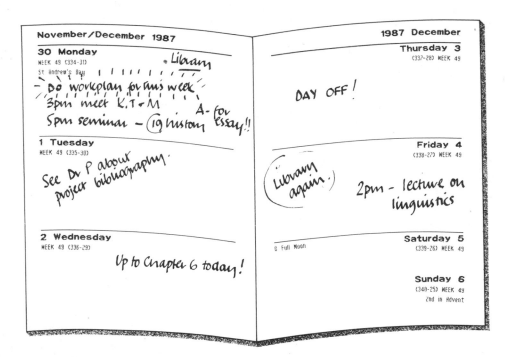

studies. You may suffer a sort of disorientation or even despair. A diary is a good way of correcting disorientation. It restores your sense of perspective by showing you where you are in terms of time and the task.

And, once again, it is an aid to learning, fixing facts.

It can even be an aid to revision. Our memories are marvellous machines but they sometimes need to be triggered, given a jolt. A four-word entry in your diary mentioning a lecture you heard a year earlier can bring back an almost verbatim recollection.

Memory-jogging You may already have noticed this memory-jogging effect in everyday life. To take a humdrum example, imagine that you have set out on a shopping expedition but when you reach the High Street you find you have left behind the shopping list you spent time and care preparing. Then you find yourself thinking: 'If only I could remember one item, I'd remember them all.' It often works. You remember 'cornflakes' and, wonder of wonders, the whole list comes back to you in a flash. The only problem is writing it all down again before you forget. Only you would not, of course, be truly forgetting – the facts would still be there in your head and it would be a matter of ferreting them out a second time. An index or diary entry can work in this way: a few words trigger a sudden flood of recollection. Indeed you may find yourself remembering not only a whole lecture but almost everything else you did on that day.

Associations Our memories work in strange ways, by making strange associations. It is a common experience to associate two otherwise totally disparate events in one's memory simply because they happened at the same time.

You are listening to a play on the radio while you are sweeping a carpet. Next day you sweep the carpet again and find that the pattern on the carpet somehow reminds you of the pattern of the play, recalling every detail of the plot, although the only real link was a brief coincidence in time. This is a clue to the way your head organises itself.

If your diary works in a similar fashion, don't fight it. You have found a way to make your head serve you better, so exploit it. The same goes for the index. Each card could be the pattern that fixes the memory and the means of recall. If you think your head works in an odd way then cash in on its quirks. By trying to change your head you may well deny your own natural talent.

There is one thing you can be quite sure of – you are a good organiser. You would not be alive if you were not capable of highly complex organisation. What you have to do is channel your power towards formal learning, using such tools as flexible plans and written records.

Just be ordinary and you'll be brilliant!

You should now be more confident about developing your own orderly learning system
●
have more ideas for organising your time
●
know how to work out priorities
●
know what aids to organisation you could use.

Finding and choosing resources

This chapter is about

how to find things out
●
using public libraries
●
other resources
available to you.

What are resources? Broadly, any person or object you can draw help from in the course of your learning. Teachers, lectures, demonstrations, books, videos – these are obvious ones, but there are others too.

First of all, how confident are you about accessing information or finding things out? Have a go at *Your access skills* opposite.

Finding out

How do you find things out in everyday life? We seek out information so often that we don't even realise we are doing it. Look at *Finding out* below.

Finding out

Write down three things you found out for the first time in the last two days. (See comments on p. 76.)

1

2

3

How did you find out each one?

1

2

3

Your access skills

Answer the questions by ticking the column that most applies to you. (See overleaf for comments.)

	Usually	Sometimes	Never
When I'm stuck and need to find something out, within five minutes or so I've thought of somewhere to look.			
I can talk face to face or over the phone with strangers if I think they can help me find out what I want to know.			
I know how to get through to the right department of large organisations.			
I try alternative approaches until I succeed in finding out what I want to know.			
Finding things out can be a challenge and I enjoy it.			
I feel confident finding out by any method.			

Write down something you would like to know or need to find out:

1 by the end of the week

2 by the end of the year

3 in the next five years

List as many ways as you can for finding out about each one.

How to find out in

a week   a year   five years

Your access skills

How did you get on?

If you answered 'usually' or 'sometimes' to most of the questions then your accessing skills are pretty good and you probably know where to find things out. But read on for more ideas.

If you answered 'never' to some of the questions then you probably need some help – which is what this chapter is for. Knowing some of the places where you can find things out should increase your confidence.

Your family

Chapter 2 looked at the possibility of your family being an obstacle, by failing to encourage you or by actually opposing your enterprise. We gave the obstructive family a hard time, but must admit that your study life may be a real nuisance to them. After all, they are the people many students will see most of; you may do all your private study under the same roof as people who previously had much more of your time and attention.

It is tactful and practical to involve your family in your study programme. It is worth repeating that people with no special knowledge of a subject can be a useful sounding-board. Any expert can be floored by an innocent question from someone who knows nothing of the topic but whose naivety has given them different insight. The best cook in the household might be stumped by a child asking: 'Why do you fry meat before putting it in a stew?' The cook may have been using the same tricks for years without knowing why and may be unable to answer a simple question like this. So if, in the course of your studies, a member of

Finding out

Any surprises? Maybe you realised that you're better at finding things out than you thought. You may also have realised that there are a great many sources of information that you can tap.

your family comes to you and asks a question you cannot answer, be thankful.

Before your family can be useful in this way, you will first have to describe your course to them from time to time, not in detail but adequately so that they have a general grasp. This way you are less likely to alienate loved ones who might otherwise feel excluded. This will directly benefit you, as well – you will probably need a non-antagonistic domestic environment for your studying to thrive. But, for some people the need to escape adverse home lives can be a spur to study.

Public libraries

How much do you know about libraries? Answer the questions in *Library quiz* below.

Library quiz

Tick the box – either true or false. Don't treat the questions too seriously!

	True	False
Students and old age pensioners pay less than others to join a public library.		✓
Only members can use the reading and study sections of the public library.		✓
Public library reference books can be borrowed for up to three weeks and read at your leisure.		✓
The librarian's main duty is to check up on the overdue books and fine their borrowers.		
Study sections in public libraries can be used for a maximum of one hour by members.		✓

To discover if your answers were correct go to your local library and find out.

Like other systems, the libraries might be even better if more money were spent on them, but they remain among the great treasure houses of every community. If you have not visited a public library lately, you may be surprised to find what unstuffy and pleasant places they are.

Libraries used to exist mainly to lend books to

people who couldn't afford to buy them, and so that people could look at periodicals and newspapers, or consult reference books in the reference section. This is still an important part of the work of a library. But larger libraries may also offer many other services:

- an information desk for finding things out
- information for local businesses
- public meetings, readings and talks
- film shows
- concerts
- talking books and larger-print books for the visually handicapped
- exhibitions of local arts and crafts, local history, etc.
- study areas
- storytelling for children
- a lending library of records, tapes and cassettes
- photocopying facilities
- refreshments
- a place where local groups can meet.

And there are many more – do you know of any?

Librarians
There to help you work through this mass of services is the librarian. Librarians are specialists who are trained in collecting, storing and finding information. If you need to find something out from a library and have trouble tracking down the right sources, ask the librarian – he or she will be able to tell you if the library has the information you want, where it is, and, if the library does not have it, where else you could try.

Librarians are there to help you – so use them!

Indexes and catalogues
Knowing how to use your library's indexes and catalogues will make your library time more interesting and more profitable.

There are three types of alphabetical index, which will be on cards or microfiche:

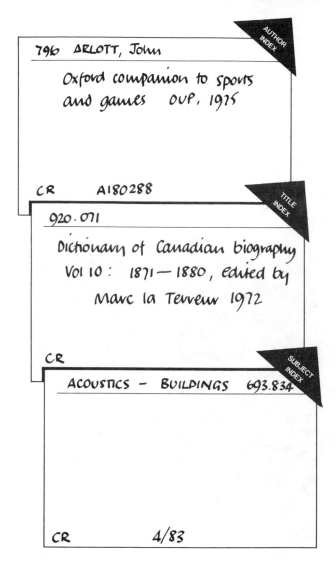

AUTHOR INDEX

796 ARLOTT, John

Oxford companion to sports
and games   OUP, 1975

CR   A180288

TITLE INDEX

920.071

Dictionary of Canadian biography
Vol 10 : 1871 — 1880, edited by
Marc la Terreur 1972

CR

SUBJECT INDEX

ACOUSTICS — BUILDINGS 693.834

CR   4/83

- by author — with their works listed
- by title — with the author's name given
- by subject — e.g. sports, cookery, theatre, etc.

  So, if you know which author you want, look in the author index; if you know which book you want but not the author's name, look in the title index.

To find information on a topic you must first find the code number for that subject. You can find this by looking in the Library Subject Index, which is probably part of the card catalogue. If there is nothing on your subject, try under a different name – for example, if you can't find anything under 'film' in the subject index you could look under 'cinema'.

Each subject has a code number which appears on the spine of the book. Books are arranged by this number on the shelf.

Cracking the code

There are ten main divisions to the code numbers. These are listed opposite. Each main division is then divided into ten major headings. We have listed the major headings of one main division, the Pure Sciences – the 500s. Each of these major headings is then divided into ten important subjects; we have chosen Physics, 530, as our example.

In Britain alone over 40 000 new titles are published every year, so don't be too surprised if the library doesn't have the book you want. Ask the librarian to obtain it for you.

Newspapers and magazines

Newspapers and magazines can be a useful part of study. If one of your goals in embarking on education is to make your life more fulfilling, quite apart from perhaps being more prosperous, then a discriminating study of what used to be called 'the public prints' is never wasted. Your subject probably has more than one regular magazine wholly devoted to it. The specialist journal field has been one of the greatest growth stories of British publishing in the past twenty years. They fall roughly into the 'professional' and the 'popular' categories. For example, *Nature* is a professional journal, most useful to research workers, and *New Scientist* a popular journal, enjoyed by general interest readers.

There are several book-form catalogues of journals. Try *British Rate and Data* (known as *BRAD*), or the *Writers' and Artists' Yearbook*.

None of the specialist magazines is designed to help

	Main Divisions				
000	General Topics				
100	Philosophy & Psychology				
200	Religion				
300	Society				
400	Languages				
500	Pure Sciences	500	Pure Sciences		
600	Technology	510	Mathematics		
700	The Arts	520	Astronomy		
800	Literature	530	Physics	530	Physics
900	Geography & History	540	Chemistry	531	Mechanics
		550	Geology	532	Mechanics of fluids
		560	Fossils	533	Mechanics of gases
		570	Biology	534	Sound
		580	Botany	535	Light
		590	Zoology	536	Heat
				537	Electricity & Electronics
				538	Magnetism
				539	Modern Physics

you pass examinations but if your day allows you time to do a little wider reading then a relevant journal will help to put your studies into a wider perspective. For example, if you are studying horticulture for a qualification to get a job in municipal gardening, you may be interested to know what is happening in the associated fields of agrochemicals, biotechnology, and so on. No subject has strict boundaries – most overlap with several others. So it can be interesting as well as rewarding for a student of fashion design to know about big changes in the oriental silkworm-farming methods, or the politics of the fur trade.

Good general knowledge is very valuable.

Which paper? A press photographer once said to a well-read friend: 'I keep meeting and photographing people who are experts and know a lot and I keep thinking how little I know. What's the best book to read to be better informed?'

The well-read friend was stumped at first. Then he said: 'There's no such book. Try reading the newspapers you work for, to start with.'

It was a good answer but it begs the question — which papers are best to read? To advise here would be to trespass on individual choice and everyone knows, anyway, that some popular papers of today are so frivolous, superficial and unreliable that reading them is likely to do more harm than good. But regular reading of a more-or-less serious newspaper will surprise you with its relevance to your studies. From catering to car mechanics, it all turns up in the daily columns, a bit less dependable than the textbooks, maybe, but with the edge of being up-to-date. Some subjects touch on almost every other subject under the sun. Think how important international politics, aeronautics, economics, psychology, geography, history, shipbuilding, trade unionism, etc., are to the holiday travel trade. The more you know about related topics, the better grasp you will have of your own speciality.

The message of this section could be put more simply but more crudely as:

**Don't waste your time reading junk.
If you are not reading course texts,
read something sensible.**

The bill Magazines and newspapers are quite expensive. A subscription to a journal can mean laying out a sizeable sum every month. Before placing a regular order, make sure of your choice by test-reading the magazine or journal at the public library. If it is not on their reading room shelves, try persuading them to buy it.

TV and radio

The old saying 'One picture is worth a thousand words' has become so hackneyed that it has lost any impact it might once have had. But it remains true that images have a special power when it comes to conveying information succinctly.

So, television should definitely be on your list of possible resources for your learning.

Study the programme listings carefully for items which might fit your needs. The same goes for radio. All networks have certain programmes tailored for students of specific subjects at different levels. Languages are particularly strong on radio, whereas mathematical formulae come over better on TV.

Do not rule out non-specialist programmes. There is a wide range of popular science programmes which

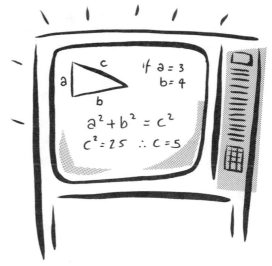

may well include something for you in the bran tub of new developments. Series like *Timewatch* touch on the history of almost all arts and sciences, with top teachers giving us the benefit of their research.

It can be a very pleasant relief from the discipline of your regular studies to let your mind scan freely over the whole horizon of information sources, and ceaselessly rewarding to discover how much stray knowledge fits into your growing grasp of a subject.

Ask a professional

Down the centuries, the word 'professional' has carried with it not only the sense of 'expert' but also of 'teacher'. The twin ideas of learning and teaching are inextricably bound together and happen simultaneously in most professions. In the academic world, the principal purpose of studying a profession is to teach it, but in the world outside the schools, the experts are still expected to be teachers. What is more, one of the most precious things about the human spirit is our deep desire to teach. The plumber may curse his apprentice, but only because he wants the youngster to learn well. Anyone who has acquired a body of useful information does not want to hoard it like a miser but to share it.

All this is good news for you. It could mean a huge bonus resource in or after your studies.

Professional organisations do not exist exclusively to protect their members from the outside world. They are there to defend their profession's reputation. They do this in several ways — by disciplining their members' conduct, by sponsoring research, by encouraging public interest and (here's where you come in) by encouraging newcomers to the field. Any professional organisation worthy of the name takes very seriously its duty to beginners or to people who are interested but have not begun at all. Some are very good at being helpful but others slip up badly when it comes to making the link between their experts and a total newcomer. They have the goodwill but lack the machinery to shake hands and say: 'Can we help you?'

So why not try crossing no man's land on your own? Take the initiative and write them a letter explaining your hopes and plans. There is nothing lost if all you get is a rebuff, and there is a good chance you will get useful guidance.

There is even an outside chance you may qualify for financial help. Some professional bodies have training trust funds set up in Victorian times or even earlier which they have almost forgotten about. Trade associations and trade unions are often equally well disposed and should definitely be checked out. The advice of any of these organisations may conflict in some respects with advice from the education system. For example, the education authority may encourage you to undertake vocational training because it is trying to fill places on a course to which it is committed, but the trade association may tend to discourage you because it feels the likelihood of eventual employment is poor. You will have to balance these two views to make your decision.

Museums

If you have been so put off by their dusty reputation that you have not visited a museum lately, then be prepared for a big surprise. Even the smallest of small town museums has been undergoing a revolution. Gone are those cobwebby cases full of dead birds with their stuffing falling out. Gone are those fossil displays that look like higgledy-piggledy heaps of gravel. Gone, too, are those indecipherable labels. So radical is the revolution that some museums even encourage visitors to TOUCH the less vulnerable items. Quite a breakthrough.

If you are on the threshold of studying a subject, whether for leisure or work, it is very likely you can find a museum with a relevant collection. Many quite small museums have displays of textiles ranging over a thousand years or more, for example. These can be very relevant if you are studying weaving or spinning or dress design. Printing, building, pharmacy, education, farming, engineering, botany, zoology . . . even quite small museums can boast useful displays of these and many more subjects.

Obviously, bigger museums may have whole departments devoted to a single speciality, such as furniture design and construction, bricklaying, lace-making, the management of water courses, animal husbandry or computer technology.

Give your museum a try. Find out about the excellent new-style museums of technology springing up around the country, led by the stunning displays at Ironbridge in Shropshire.

Using museums as a resource has a double value to

you. A good display first of all teaches you about the subject, but it also stirs in you a pride in its history and a greater wish to be part of it. For example, the history of town drainage down the centuries may sound a dingy study but is in fact quite dramatic, even romantic! Anyone who has read A. J. Cronin's novel *The Citadel* about a young doctor's fight for better sewers will appreciate the drama of drains. A visit to a museum display on the subject could spur you to study.

You should now
have an idea of the
range of resources
available to you
●
be more confident
about using libraries.

5

Reading and note-taking

You may think, like many people, that technological changes are making reading less important. But TV, video, computers and fast forms of communication have not made reading redundant. Far from it: evi-

dence suggests that, far from declining, the ability to read has never been more important than it is now.

Skilled reading = power!

If you can read

• quickly

• selectively

• accurately

then you will have more access to information and ideas.

Spend some time thinking about what reading involves.

Patterns of meaning

For a start, reading is not the same as writing – they are not part of the same brain activity. You may well know people who are good at reading but poor at writing.

There is more to reading than understanding the meaning of particular words. In fact individual letters, syllables, words and phrases do not mean much in isolation. Imagine an American Indian reading smoke signals. Each puff has no meaning by itself. A pattern of meaning emerges only when the signals are seen in relation to each other. And a slight difference in sequence can make a huge difference: 'I want a horse chestnut' does not mean the same as 'I want a chestnut horse'! The meaning of the sentence depends on the word order.

When transferring spoken language into writing we retain all manner of props and devices which may have been useful in speech but are less important on the page. Our brains ignore them – we quickly spot an irrelevancy and skip it.

It is easy to skip and guess because we are familiar with certain combinations of words.

Try this:

> *Learning —— a natural human activity which all —— us do all our lives. We never stop. As children we learn —— waik, talk, understand where —— are, and what everything around us —— for; as adults —— learn many new skills. Learning—not something you only do —— school.*

You will probably guess the meaning correctly in spite of the gaps in the evidence. Your brain uses its knowledge of the possible meanings of each word or group of words and the context of the text as a whole.

Now try this:

> *The only —— between normal everyday learning and being —— or trained is that in the second case you do it self-consciously, on purpose. But learning is a set of —— you can —— to be better at, by doing —— skills courses or reading books about it. There is a —— of relevant—to help you.*

This time you probably found it much more difficult, though the number of words to predict was the same.

In the first exercise the predictions were easier because the missing words were unimportant on their own, they simply linked the more important words together, and are called 'link' words for that reason. In the second exercise the meaning of the passage depended on the missing words – the 'meaning-carriers'.

Now, working with a partner, each choose a passage from a magazine or book. Delete as many words as you can without losing the sense of the passage. Now exchange passages and see if your partner can still make out the sense. Which did you delete – link words or meaning-carrier words?

You may also have found that you can predict some meaning-carriers if the context is strong enough. For example, look at this sentence:

'Would you like a cup of ———?'

You probably guessed tea or coffee.

Vocabulary   Although we may need a vocabulary of several tens of thousands of words to enjoy full communication with one another, only 100 words make up 50 per cent of speech and writing. They are the link words – 'the', 'and', 'but' and so on.

Writing, however, is a slow process. It is characterised by precision, compared with the broadness of speech. There is much more work for your mind to do when writing. It has to find the words to match the thought, spell the words and set them down. Spelling takes an effort not required in speech or reading.

A matter of mood   Information cannot be poured into the human mind like water into a jug. The mind has its moods and if you pick up a book, read its contents and expect your memory to hold the whole lot without preparation then you risk a disappointment. You need to get into the right frame of mind first. Everyone knows how easily we can make a hash of something as simple as cleaning a bicycle or making a cake if we fail first to

Be prepared

Think about preparation by describing how you could best spend up to ten minutes preparing to read, listen to or watch something.

1　Jot down what you are hoping to learn about, in one or two sentences. For example, you could put:

After doing this I should be able to describe......

and fill in, say, three things. Afterwards, check whether you were able to or not. If not, what else happened?

2　Jot down up to five important things you already know about the subject. If you only know a bit, it should be easy. If you already know a lot, you will have to make a selection.

3　If possible, talk to someone about what you expect to learn. Afterwards, review what you actually learned.

manoeuvre our minds into the right mood for the task, quite apart from assembling the tools and materials. This is just as true of reading a book. It is true, too, of your approach to lectures or watching a TV programme. Dashing from place to place and then plonking yourself down in front of a lecturer at the last moment is not only rude to the lecturer but unfair to yourself. Give your head a chance to get its act together.

Many people find that a useful technique in preparing for reading is to think about what they expect to learn from the text. They try to make deductions from what they already know about the course and the title of the book or chapter. That way, they can send a mental scout ahead, exploring the landscape on the other side of the hill. If you use this technique, then make notes and, if possible, talk to someone about what you think the text holds for you. Try to be specific. If you already know a fair amount about what you are going to read, then jot down half a dozen points. Keep these notes and, when you have read the book or chapter, compare your expectations with what really happened. Quite apart from its value in getting you into the right frame of mind, this process helps you realise the pace of your own advance. Once we have learned something we tend to have the feeling it has been part of us for ages and is common knowledge anyway. By making notes in advance of reading, we are setting up milestones as reminders of what we did not know before we marched ahead. You can use the same 'scouting' technique when going to hear a lecture.

How much? Another widespread misconception is that to get what you want from a book you have to read the whole of it.

It is not a sign of laziness or lack of diligence to read only those parts of a book which seem most likely to be useful. Reading too much in too little time may clog up your brain and slow down your learning.

It is better to scan the text first, digest the index, read the first and final chapters, get a feel of the whole work. Then you know enough to begin dipping into the text. Dipping is not cheating. You are not in a competition to read as many books as you can. You are merely spending time wisely. Trust your selectivity. If you attempt to read everything word by word you may well be ground down by the enormity of the task and lose heart.

Skimming When you skim a page (or a chapter) you get an idea of what it's about. You do not read every word but instead you read:

- the title and subheadings

- the first sentence from each paragraph (or the first paragraph of the chapter)

- the last sentence of the passage (or the last paragraph of the chapter).

If the chapter you are reading contains a summary, you should read that first. You should pay attention to any diagrams, charts or graphs.

Skimming the cream

Skim the passage first and then answer the questions that follow.

Energy
Everything that happens involves energy; either it is released, or it is taken in. The sun provides most of the energy which is used on earth.

Forms of energy
There are many, including:
    chemical
    kinetic
    nuclear
    heat
    electrical
    sound
    light
    potential.

Energy can be stored in the form of chemical, nuclear or potential energy but it is harder to store in other forms.

Energy changes
One form of energy can be changed into another. For example, if you clap your hands, chemical energy stored in your muscles is converted to movement and then to sound. When you travel in a car and the brakes are applied, movement energy is converted to heat in the brakes. Machines can control the amount of energy released and how much useful work it does.

1   The passage is about ....

2   There are approximately ...... forms of energy.

3   Machines are devices which ....

Scanning the page

Scan this periodic table of elements to see if gold (Au) is amongst them.

H																	He
Li	Be											B	C	N	O	F	Ne
Na	Mg											Al	Si	P	S	Cl	Ar
K	Ca	Sc	Ti	V	Cr	Mn	Fe	Co	Ni	Cu	Zn	Ga	Ge	As	Se	Br	Kr
Rb	Sr	Y	Zr	Nb	Mo	Tc	Ru	Rh	Pd	Ag	Cd	In	Sn	Sb	Te	I	Xe
Cs	Ba	La	Hf	Ta	W	Re	Os	Ir	Pt	Au	Hg	Tl	Pb	Bi	Po	At	Rn

Now scan the passage 'The World under Water' so that you can fill in the missing words in the three sentences. Read the sentences first.

1 If the world's ice melted the level of the sea would rise by _____ m.

2 The Antarctic summer would be _____ than the Arctic but its winters would be more _____.

3 During the warmer phases in the early part of this century some types of fish suddenly appeared off the _____ coast.

The World under Water

Since one tenth of the world is covered by ice the effect on mankind if all the ice melted would be dramatic. Most of this ice stretches across the 1,800,000 sq km (700,000 sq miles) of Greenland and the 13,000,000 sq km (5,000,000 sq miles) of Antarctica. If all this ice were to melt the level of the seas would rise by about 76 metres (250 feet) swamping all the world's harbours and many of its principal cities. The Panama Canal would become a strait and the Suez Canal would vanish. The Bering Strait between Alaska and the USSR would widen, allowing more warm water to sweep into the Arctic and channelling cold water down to the west coast of America. Most of southern England would vanish apart from the Cotswolds, Mendips, Chilterns and Downs. Only the tips of the New York skyscrapers would peep above the waves but Australia and Africa would be relatively unharmed. Rainfall would be redistributed and Continental areas could experience drought. Such a melting could shift the poles and start another Ice Age due to more water vapour – and hence more snow.

But, apart from the submerging of vast areas of land, the effect would be a return to the conditions experienced just before the great Ice Ages. Air temperatures in both high and low latitudes would be very similar. The temperature of the Arctic would rise by 5–10°C in summer and by 2.5–5°C in winter. The Antarctic summer would be warmer than the Arctic but its winters would be more severe. There could even be a return to sub-tropical vegetation in the lower latitudes and there would be mass migrations of birds and animals towards the north. The warming of the sea would have a pronounced effect on the pattern of sea life. For example, during the warmer phase of the early part of this century the cod, herring and haddock suddenly appeared off the Greenland coast. As the climate became cooler in the 1960s, the catch dropped dramatically. In some land areas there would be a big increase in the agricultural growing season.

(From Collins' *Young Scientist* by M. Ketzner)

Scanning When you scan a page or chapter, you are looking for a piece of information. You do not need to read every word but instead you should run your eye down the page fairly quickly.

Pressing on regardless You do not need to read a book as if it were some sort of obstacle race in which you are forbidden to proceed until you have surmounted everything in your path. If you simply fail to grasp what a writer is driving at in a course book, there is no need to hang around struggling with the problem. Set it aside. Make a note that you have done so. But press on. Something later in the same text may provide a vital clue, enabling you to go back and read the puzzling paragraphs with new eyes. More important, by pressing on you are more likely to keep the thread of what the text is trying to tell you. If you get the broad picture, you can focus on the blurred bits later.

Sometimes, if we are having difficulty with a text, we get rattled and begin to be intimidated by the task. A symptom of this is if we find ourselves proceeding very slowly, forcing ourselves to ponder every word and make sure we grasp its full meaning. This could be a sign that the fearful side of our make-up is playing tricks with us. All this fussing around over single words is really dawdling in order to avoid the real effort. But so often this fearfulness springs from that same mistaken belief that it is cheating to skim and dip and even skip over obstacles. Do not let yourself get bogged down in futile plodding from word to word. If you really want to read that way, then do it later. Much later. After you have boldly read on regardless, seeking for signs of the shape of the ideas the writer wants you to know about.

Selecting Some books, though, may be unsuitable for your purpose. Go through *Select/Reject* overleaf to try out one approach to finding the right book.

Browsing It seems curious, but idle reading or browsing can be a very active and effective way of learning. The information is coming to you at a time when you are not

Select/Reject

- Make sure the book is not too difficult for you; if the first page has more than five words you do not understand then it probably is.

- If you need up-to-date information then check the book's date of publication – you'll find this on the back of the title page.

- See if the book has a summary at the end of each chapter or a conclusion at the end of the book. These can save you time. If there is no summary then read the first and last paragraph of each relevant chapter to help you decide if you will need to use it.

Where would you look to see if a book:

1 Had an illustration you wanted?

2 Had a qualified author you could quote?

3 Was up-to-date?

4 Had general information on your topic?

5 Had a particular piece of information you were seeking? E.g. the name of an inventor.

bullying your brain with the command: 'Remember, remember!' Browsing also seems to open the mind up more freely to make associations in a creative way. You may, at times like this, stumble across the delightful fact that you already possess a body of knowledge which you had never thought relevant to your present studies until this moment. If that happens, you are fortunate, but in any event, browsing is not an idle activity. The trouble is, once you start to organise browsing, it tends to lose its charm.

Reading strategies   Look at *Reading strategies* opposite to see whether you agree with the explanations of these five methods.

Through other eyes   In reading as in every other activity mentioned so far, the virtue of having someone to talk to about your study can scarcely be overemphasised. Remind yourself that this does not need to be an expert in your chosen subject. Any alert, well-disposed individual's view is worth hearing, and a friend who will sometimes play quite a passive role as a sounding-board is very valuable. It can be astonishing how a problem in your reading, which has been going round and round

Reading strategies

Method	Description	Purpose
Detailed reading:	means reading the whole passage carefully and thoughtfully – though this doesn't have to be slowly.	Complete understanding
Reading for enjoyment:	means reading at whatever pace suits you. The more you read the better you become at reading.	Pleasure
Skimming:	means finding out what a chapter or book is mainly about.	General impression
Scanning:	means looking for specific detail by running your eye down the page quickly.	Fact-finding
Detecting bias:	means that some people (advertisers, politicians) write to persuade, so you need to separate fact from opinion.	Making up your own mind

in your head but remains baffling, can resolve itself in the act of talking about it to someone else.

Note-taking

Understanding how we use language can help us make more useful notes. Useful notes taken while reading may well include thoughts which are not in the text but spring from your own conclusions. The purpose of your notes is to act as a reminder of what you have read. A few key words will trigger your memory better than long sentences. Remind yourself all the time of what you are trying to achieve, what you will want to remember in six months' time.

The test of any note-taking system is: does it work? If it works for you stick with it, even if other people say it is a mess. But do not close your mind to other people's ways of doing things. They may hold a valuable hint for you. You may adapt your system in the light of others. But in the early stages of your study you need to fix on a method of making notes that settles down into a regular framework of headings, subheadings, cross-references, highlighting and so on.

But if you are sharing the note-taking with other students, you will have to match your structures.

Comparing notes

Compare these two examples of notes:

Example 1

Blood is a mixture of red, white cells
plasma, platelets. Red cells carry O made
in bodies. White cells kill germs.
Platelets clot blood. Heart pumps bd
around body.
Arteries main tubes leading
from H. Thick walls. End of art
called capillaries — fine tubes water
moves food.
O to cells and gets waste
away. Tissue fluid. Veins carry O
back to H. His two pumps, one bigger
than other. Heart has one way ↗ valves
Heart beats to pump bd — Nerves controlled
beats of heart.

right
atrium

left
atrium

right
ventrical

left
ventrical

Example 2

BLOOD contains

RED CELLS : contain haemoglobin which
carries oxygen.

WHITE CELLS : digests germs + produces
antibodies.

PLATELETS : clot blood when tissue is cut.
PLASMA : mainly water, transports
all the above + other chemicals.

ARTERIES : carries high pressure blood
away from heart (Ht). thick
walls.

VEINS : carry returning blood to heart.
CAPILLARIES : end of Art. fine tubes.

O2 and food pass through
watery fluid called
TISSUE FLUID to cells.
Waste and CO2 go other way.

Use a red pen to circle any weak points in these notes. Use a blue pen to tick strong points. Which are most similar to your notes?

Most students make notes but many do this without really thinking about why they are making them. Why should you bother? (You should be able to think of more than one reason.)

Methods of making notes

'The more the merrier' is certainly not a good rule in note-taking. The more notes you take, the more difficult they will be to use later. Be economical and make them well organised. Try to boil down a whole section of a book into a single sentence. The very process of paraphrasing a text can fix it in your memory and make comprehension easier, so avoid copying out whole sentences word for word. Unless your notes mean something to you as you write them, they will mean little when you use them for revision.

The ability to pick out key words for your notes is very valuable.

Key words

Key words are the ones which are most loaded with meaning, the ones that unlock your memory.

Read this passage to find out why Britain has a standard railway gauge of 4 ft 8.5 in (1.435 m). Underline the key words to help you.

At the beginning of the nineteenth century most of the freight wagons in use on the coalfields of northern England had a distance of 4 ft 8.5 in between their wheels. As the railway system developed this odd distance became standard for the gauge of much of the track in England and indeed in the world.

Railway companies were then private enterprises and many of them centred their activities around two major towns or cities. The companies quickly realised that to link up track was to their mutual advantage and so the 4 ft 8.5 in gauge, or 'narrow gauge', spread southward beyond Birmingham.

When Isambard Kingdom Brunel was pioneering the Great Western Railway (running westward from Paddington in London) he helped to design track, engines and carriages. He was a very competent and accomplished engineer, and he calculated that space for passengers and freight, stability and speed (through the use of larger engines) would all be best served by using a 7 ft gauge for his track. He put his ideas into practice and laid broad gauge from London to Penzance.

Brunel's railway was joined to the broad-gauge Bristol and Gloucester line and it linked to the narrow-gauge Birmingham and Gloucester line at Gloucester. This junction was chaotic and uneconomic and caused the Midland Railway to open its narrow-gauge line right through from Birmingham to Bristol. The public began to take sides. A Royal Commission opened in 1845 to investigate the matter.

Contests were arranged to impress the commission with speed and with tonnage carried. Despite several notable victories by Brunel and his team the Commission decided in favour of narrow gauge. Brunel fought on bitterly but it was felt that the 1900 miles (3057 km) of narrow gauge should be left alone and the 274 miles (441 km) of broad gauge should be narrowed. It was, of course, much cheaper to reduce track in width than to broaden it. The last broad-gauge train left Paddington on 20 May 1892.

The battle of the gauges accelerated progress in the design of railway engines. However, any engineer founding a railway today would far prefer a broad gauge to the standard 4 ft 8.5 in gauge for the same reasons that influenced Brunel.

Now write a headline to sum up what the passage is about. Choose your headline from your key words. You can practise by picking out key words when you are reading your own newspaper.

Making notes from lectures can present problems unless the lecturer knows how to be helpful. It is difficult for the student to know which parts of a lecture will emerge as the most important until the lecture has been completed. But a good lecturer will declare his or her intentions at the outset, proceed with the lecture and then sum up at the end. This way, the student does not feel lost. If your lecturer is poor at giving you the advance structure of the lecture, then you may be able to change things. Suggest that it would be helpful to you and your colleagues if the main headings of the lecture were written up or projected on a screen so that you can all chart your way through.

Be alert for changes of topic within the lecture. These will provide you with your main headings.

Before starting to take notes on a chapter, scan ahead to see what subheadings the text uses. These could well serve as your own note headings. If you attempt to impose a single set of your own headings on every text you tackle, they will probably quite often turn out to be inappropriate. You could end up with a heading over a blank space because the text contained nothing that would fit. There is a true story of an author who was engaged to write the volume about Iceland in a series of books about the world's wildlife. The publishers gave him a list of headings to which he was compelled to adhere. So when he came to the stipulated section called 'Owls', he simply wrote: 'There are no owls in Iceland.' Don't get into such a twist yourself!

Some people like using clusters or sprays as a method of note-taking. Take a look at *Sprays* and *Pattern notes* opposite.

Abbreviations Clear and accurate abbreviations (Abvs) are used widely to save time and space when writing notes. Sometimes the words or phrases which are used frequently in a book or article are written out at the beginning and then abbreviated afterwards.

Some students write notes with connecting words missing. Saves time + space, but be careful when reading notes, interpret accurately.

Sprays

Sprays are a way of quickly jotting down all your ideas on a subject and linking them up. They save time because you don't have to write sentences or put words down in any particular order.

Stage 1: putting the words down

Stage 2: making the links

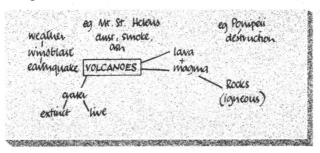

Now make your own spray about a topic you are interested in.

Pattern notes

If you want to keep your notes and use them later you need to organise them. Pattern notes are a very effective way of planning an essay or of preparing a summary of a section of work. They are an absorbing and fruitful method of revising.

Look at the pattern note on *Choosing a place to live* and notice the use of space, lettering, key words, and the way they have linked ideas together. You can make effective use of colour too.

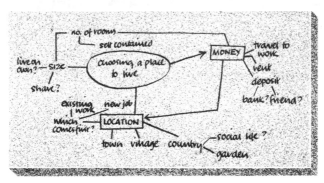

Now make your own pattern note on a subject you are studying or something you are interested in.

Another method of abbreviating notes is to leave out all the vowels: ths s stll srprsngly smpl t rd.

In short

You probably know more abbreviations than you think. Note down the meaning of these abbreviations and symbols.

=	≠	+
%	@	&
—	×	etc.
$	÷	.
∴	∵	♂
♀	NB	i.e.
"	e.g.	C17
cm	kg	s

Write down any other abbreviations that you know, or any of your own that you could use in your work.

Equipment It is worth getting your note-taking equipment right, too. A loose-leaf system, using a ring-binder or some similar method, is by far the best. If you use a permanently bound notebook you will have to anticipate at the outset how much space you expect to need for each section and this is almost impossible to get right. If you have a whole series of books for each section the whole system becomes cumbersome and less use for revision. So stick to the loose-leaf binder. One of its advantages, apart from its being easily expanded at any point, is that keeping contents pages becomes easier. And keeping contents pages, apart from being an aid to revision, is once again a means of committing to memory.

The loose-leaf system will in addition encourage you to spread yourself on the page. You will not feel obliged to cram notes together to save space. Well-spaced notes are a great deal easier to understand. The whole art of typography down the centuries has been directed not only to elegance but to comprehensibility, so be your own typographer. A further advantage of well-spaced notes is that they make additions easier.

Putting it into practice

Although you are aiming at brevity and clarity, your notes do not have to be bleak. Use any trick you think will work for you to fix ideas and make them accessible in revision. Use drawings, lists, memory-jogging mnemonics, even jokes – anything that is effective. These notes are you talking to yourself so it does not much matter what other people make of them, unless, that is, you are working in a note-taking team with others. The team approach, as we have mentioned before, can work wonderfully well but it demands extra self-control.

Do not be daunted by the size of the job or other people's apparent superiority. You have on your side a well-developed ability to comprehend your own language. Now you must learn to set it down in notes in a way that enables you to speak to yourself. Good notes are an aid to fixing information in your memory as well as triggering information later.

You should now
know about some different reading skills and how you can use them

•

have practised a few reading techniques

•

know the main uses of note-taking and some different ways to go about it.

6

Thinking about thought

Serious thinking has a bad reputation: it is seen as gloomy, self-indulgent and hard work. This is nonsense. The sort of thought demanded by serious study can be exhilarating, liberating and richly rewarding, even if the subject is quite humdrum. It can be a wonderful surprise to discover what our heads can achieve when given the chance.

The power to think

Earlier chapters examined your innate capacity to learn and to organise – two talents you may well have doubted you possessed. The power to think purposively is a similar case.

However muddled and cloudy your thinking may seem to you, you undoubtedly possess the power to give it direction for the purposes of study and to understand. With learning and organising we need to harness the power we already possess and practise. We can do the same with thought.

There is much satisfaction to be gained from the exercise for its own sake. Physical exercise can be a great pleasure – there is something similar to be had from thought. To feel we are getting to the bottom of a subject takes methodical work but we are aided all the way by the natural activity of our mind.

Sudden perceptions   If you trust as well as train your mind it will sometimes give you sudden perceptions which are the sheer pleasure of thought and of learning.

It can happen in a flash at a time when you are in despair over your own failure to comprehend. For example, you may have been a diligent student of history, learning every fact you are offered about a particular period but, at the same time, wondering why that period in history matters so much, why the course gives it so much space, why your teacher is making such a fuss about it. Then, quite suddenly and rather to your surprise, your mind gives you a glimpse of the whole era, its scientists, artists and politicians, its workers and clergy. All the elements were there in your head but in separate bubbles. But it took a leap of imagination to 'see' a whole society. The sudden vision may have been unbidden but you did all the work to make it possible by first studying each element. We cannot promise that every course of study will produce moments quite as rewarding as this, but there is no real reason why it should not.

The study of mathematics is famous for bringing sudden perceptions to its students – the workings of elaborate machinery can be baffling at one moment and plain the next. Even someone with no technological training can find it rewarding suddenly to grasp the essential difference between a jet engine and a rocket.

How this happens is open to speculation. It is the province of psychologists, philosophers and several other sorts of scientists. But we do not need to understand our thought processes in order to harness them.

105

Edward De Bono in his many books has shown how we can all successfully set our minds to tasks by using logical techniques. If you are interested in knowing more about his work, check the Booklist.

You versus you

what are you trying to tell me?

The use of techniques to channel our minds towards exploring a certain subject can be a simple art. For example, try conducting a formal debate in your head. Take several sides in the argument. Contradict your own first opinions. Spend time working out ways to prove that your most passionately held convictions could be baseless. Be your own most fervent opponent. If your dearest beliefs can stand up to stringent examination and survive intact, then you may understand them better, or perhaps understand them truly for the first time.

A precious by-product of this process is that it encourages a generally questioning frame of mind, a sensible tendency to take nothing at face value, even the solemn assurances of a trusted teacher.

Challenging popular views

Another useful exercise is to challenge ideas which may not be your own but which are popularly held views. Every generation has its almost unquestioned verities which are promptly overturned by the next. Until fairly recent times a long period of formal mourning was considered necessary to the healing process; now the bereaved are reminded that 'Life must go on' and 'Tears won't bring back the dead'. This sort of social somersault is quite common.

Trying to prove the earth is really flat might be asking too much, but how about the widely held notion that if you obey the law yourself it will encourage others to do the same? And does travel really broaden the mind?

Exercises like these establish a habit of questioning – this is a valuable state of mind. There is even a virtue in being in sharp disagreement with your teacher or your course material. This is not because it enhances your sense of individuality or is good for your ego but because it seems to create a heightened awareness which will help you understand and remember. From being the passive receptor of facts, you have turned yourself into an active seeker after truth. You have a stake in the matter and that fixes its shape in your head. In the end you may well fall into agreement with your teacher or the author of your course material, but you will have been through the process of challenge and that will have done the trick.

Act it out

Here is another simple hint for using your mind – do not assume the process of thought is necessarily distinct from physical activity. Thought need not be something going on in your head with no outward manifestation. Head and hand can study together in ways an onlooker might find quite comical. For example, if you are studying a subject which requires physical skill, try miming its actions.

The manoeuvres needed to operate a huge JCB earth mover with precision are very demanding on head and hand. Although a student carpenter has some hope of practising at home, the JCB driver can scarcely park the machine in the back garden and have a trial run on the cabbage patch. What the driver can do, however, is mime the operation of the controls. It may seem a little odd to sit there, pulling imaginary levers, but it is a perfectly valid way of using head and hands together to learn.

Going through the motions

When did you last act something out to help your understanding? Perhaps you can think of several occasions. Write down what you were simulating, how you did it, and whether it helped or not.

What   *How*   *Did it help?*

Try this aid to understanding whenever you can – it could help you fix things in your mind.

Use your imagination To help your mime, use your imaginative powers to put yourself in the situation you are miming. Try to see yourself abseiling, swimming, driving – whatever.

Visualise as clearly as you can what it would actually feel like. What sensations are there in your body? How will you move your hands and feet? What do your surroundings look like, and what are you wearing? Are you scared/elated, confident/insecure?

Give it a go – it could well concentrate your mind on the mime. And if it helps your understanding of what's involved in the activity it will be highly profitable – you may also find it quite good fun.

Even abstractions can be helped by miming. Imagine a family trying to resolve a dispute over where to take a holiday. They face many permutations of possibilities involving money, personal tastes, timings, availability and locations. The whole issue becomes so complicated that the family tries to clarify things by sitting round the dinner table and using the salt, mustard, pepper, butter, cutlery and place mats as tokens to represent people and places.

Quite complex concepts can be made clearer by using hands as well as heads. Risk feeling ridiculous and give it a try!

Demonstrating Try demonstrating a mime to one of your mentors – a mime you have used to help you understand and learn something. It could be really useful – an innocent question from your mentor about your mime could clarify things in your own mind.

Be your instructor

We have just recommended adopting a role and arguing with yourself. We have also recommended literally going through the motions of a physical or abstract technique. Now try combining the two and putting yourself in the position of your own instructor. Acting out the role is a remarkably effective way of getting to grips with a tricky subject.

What has happened is that, once again, you have played an active role in the learning process, raised the temperature a little, and in this way created a favourable state of mind.

An extra lesson can be drawn from this exercise – instructors may not be quite as learned as you had assumed. You may find you can swot up on a topic and give a convincing lecture, which is exactly what many teachers do at the very last minute before entering the classroom. Sometimes a teacher is only a pace ahead of the students. This is not necessarily disreputable. The only test is that old question: does it work? If the technique works, use it.

Logical thinking

Often a problem can be solved or a proposition understood by a logical examination. This may sound obvious, but it is surprising how often we will nibble all round the edges of a problem instead of boldly breaking it up into its elements.

Start by identifying the problem itself. This may be by no means as simple as it sounds. We all tend to jump to conclusions in our haste to solve problems, especially if we are under pressure.

Consider the predicament of a young mother driving a car through a remote area on a very cold night. She has as her only passenger her very small baby. Suddenly the car breaks down. She fears for the baby's safety and decides her first priority is to get the car repaired so that she can take the baby home. So she applies her mind to ways to repair the car. But another way of analysing her problem suggests that her first priority is keeping herself and the baby warm; the car is incidental.

By giving the car repairs top priority she may have ruled out options such as finding other shelter and lighting a fire. This rather dramatic example shows that defining the problem can be a problem in itself. So one early item on your problem-solving check-list might be:

- What is the problem?

Then try:

- What are the options?

- What is in favour of each option?

- What is against each option?

- What information do I lack?

By using a method as simple as this you may soon find out that certain aspects of the situation which had loomed large have now dwindled in importance.

Information It is worth emphasising the importance of the last item in that brief check-list: information. It is very easy to slip into the habit of assuming a problem has to be solved in the way it has been presented.

But in the real world we need to come up with real, workable solutions. So your questioning approach should extend to asking whether you know enough to make a rational decision and whether other relevant information is available before you decide. Remind yourself yet again that you are the boss.

Try out our check-list to see if it works for you. See *Problem-solving* opposite.

Making comparisons To that first brief list could be added at least one more step in problem-solving or decision-making: the search for analogies. Contrive or recall a situation

Problem-solving

Apply the five-point check-list to a recent problem you have had to sort out. Jot down brief notes under each of the headings:

The problem

The options

Points in favour of each option

Points against each option

Information needed

Did you find it useful for analysing the problem? Did it make you see the problem differently? Would you have made a different decision if you'd used this check-list in the first place?

which was similar. The outcome of the analogous situation might unlock the solution to your present problem.

Someone trying to solve a town's traffic jams might in an analogy visualise the vehicles as water running through canals and locks to see if that helps towards a solution. A bit far-fetched, but worth a try.

Advantages, risks and issues

A variation on the five-point check-list invites you first to write down the choices open to you and then to ask yourself what are the

- advantages
- risks
- issues.

Take the imaginary example of a promising young engineer who is also a good footballer. Before completing his engineering training he is offered a full-time job as a professional player with a not very

successful local team. He finds both careers highly attractive. How does he analyse his problem?

First, he looks at the engineering option.

Advantages: It is a secure, prosperous and interesting career.

Risks: He might fail to get his qualifications. He might find engineering dull as a lifetime's work.

Issues: His father was an engineer and wants his son to follow the family tradition. His girlfriend works at the same engineering factory.

Next, the footballing option.

Advantages: He enjoys football more than training as an engineer. He would be paid more at first and so could pay the debts that are worrying him.

Risks: The offer comes from a poor team who may train him badly. He would have to be brilliant to transfer to a better team. Footballers' careers are short.

Issues: His father would be disappointed. He would see less of his girlfriend.

A decision like this would undoubtedly have more elements than those presented here and certain aspects, such as the relative importance of pleasing other people, are matters for personal judgement. But if the problem-solver can at least write down the pros and cons and plonk a side-issue label on elements that are not central to the discussion, then he or she will certainly have made some progress. On the facts we have here, what do you think the engineer/footballer should do?

Try out the format on a problem of your own. Look at *Analysing the options* overleaf.

Concentrating

At the beginning of this chapter we noted how thought has a gloomy image. People tend to see thinking as some sort of mental drudgery, rather than a liberating activity. Perhaps this mistaken view of thinking springs from our early schooldays when we were told, 'Concentrate and pay attention.' Concentrating seemed to entail furrowed brows and a degree of physical tension. So we dutifully furrowed our brows and crouched over our exercise books to show how hard we were concentrating.

It was all a sham. Real concentration does not involve frowns and hunched shoulders. On the contrary, someone engrossed in a subject is probably in a

Analysing the options

Now try the advantages, risks, issues format for a problem of your own. It could be a recent problem, or even one you are still working out.

Fill in the chart:

OPTION:

_____

Advantages:

_____

Risks:

_____

Issues:

_____

OPTION:

_____

Advantages:

_____

Risks:

_____

Issues:

_____

OPTION:

_____

Advantages:

_____

Risks:

_____

Issues:

_____

Has this helped you at all? You may have found it hard to slice up the problem in this way – it often is. But if you use the format frequently, it will become easier.

state of relaxation. When we enter into this condition of mental activity it is curiously close to play. It is a paradox that a child's mental activity in the playground can be closer to true concentration than it ever is in the classroom where brows are furrowed fraudulently.

The joke is that it takes more effort to act out the role of the thinker than actually to think. A soldier sentenced to labour in the kitchens as punishment for some misdemeanour may apply himself to evading the punishment by only pretending to work. He will pick up a mop and walk about industriously without actually mopping the floor. He hopes his idleness will not be noticed. But he has to work so hard at getting away with being idle that it would have been easier to mop the floor.

It can be the same with thinking. If we believe that by adopting the conventional appearances of thought we will achieve anything worthwhile we are deceiving ourselves.

A wandering mind   Odd as it may sound, the process of concentrating can entail letting your mind wander. For creative thinking is a little like juggling. The more balls you can get in the air, the greater the chance of seeing new patterns emerge. The mind needs to draw on its many sources, from past experience as well as recent instruction.

Consciously, you can point your mind in a certain direction, but you cannot hope to steer it every step of the way, nor should you try. It is in the very nature of thought and creativity to embrace a certain randomness.

As an analogy to demonstrate our need for randomness, the writer Arthur Koestler drew attention to a laboratory experiment. In the experiment, a person's eyes were fixed on a stationary object by a mechanical device. It might be thought that such a device would enable the person to concentrate on the object without letting his attention wander. But what in fact happened was that the image of the object disintegrated and disappeared altogether before reappearing after a while in a fragmentary or distorted form. Koestler went on to draw an analogy between physical vision with the eyes and purely mental perception. He concluded that static vision does not exist and that there is no seeing without exploring.

In other words, he was saying that our minds need to scan just as our eyes do. Total concentration is alien to our mental process and actually harmful.

Whatever the truth of Koestler's ideas may be, think about it – the wider the channel in which you can let your thoughts flow, the better your head may work. Certainly you can safely rid yourself of the frowns and furrows of the classroom.

You may not be treated to the sort of sudden insight which allowed Newton to conceive the nature of gravity or Cambridge scientists to see the double helix of DNA, but give your mind credit for the power it has.

Archimedes made his discovery about the nature of the physical world – which was a leap forward for mankind – while he was relaxing in his bath. There was nothing narrow about the way Archimedes thought!

Distractions

All this is not to deny that many thoughts which enter your head while you are studying really can be distracting and harmful.

One of the causes of failure to concentrate adequately is the very fear of not concentrating. You may be lumbered with that image we have mentioned before of someone sitting with hunched shoulders and a furrowed brow, and feel that you're not genuinely concentrating unless you look like that for long periods of time.

The truth is that concentration may come in comparatively short spasms which grow longer as you become accustomed to study and feel increasingly at ease. Groundless anxiety blocks the tranquillity of study, so try to keep a sense of proportion about distractions. With time and goodwill you can hope to feel so at home in your personal world of learning that your concentration becomes far better than you ever expected.

Liberation

One final point in this brief exploration of thinking and creativity: Solomon was right, there is nothing new under the sun. It is not given to any of us to create something entirely new. Everything we do is derived to some extent from things other people have done before us. In engineering as in the arts, we are individuals in a long line of human endeavour. When your instructors are lecturing, they are trying to hand down the hard-won wisdom of others. If you are fortunate, you may even add to the process. But merely to share in the great traffic of knowledge is a pleasure in itself quite apart from its application. You will indeed find that thought is not drudgery but liberation.

You should now
have tried out some
tricks to help your
learning
•
have more ideas for
thinking a problem
through
•
know more about
concentration.

117

Writing

The world has about 5000 languages and dialects. The majority of them are probably of limited value for the expression of ideas on science, commerce and the arts. Of those 5000, English has the biggest vocabulary. It has 800000 words, any 60000 of which may be commanded by a competent individual. English is a goldmine in common ownership yet it is often regarded as more of a threat than a resource. Possessors of this precious language can feel anxious at having to attempt a piece of sustained writing.

Why does writing in English bring out such inhibitions among people who speak it fluently and effectively? Perhaps we have still not shaken off the legacy of those grim grammarians who taught English as a rigid structure of rules and regulations, rather than inviting us to explore its richness and exuberance. Perhaps this applies to any language.

On the other hand some people feel so confident about writing that they are lured into traps. They tend to write English in such a high-flown and complex style that it defies easy understanding. The trouble is, those among us who lack confidence in our writing sometimes try to imitate them. An extreme is gobbledegook like this:

> *By a process of analytic and practical reductions the problem of differential opportunity under welfarism is divested of its structure in order thus to be transposed on to various psycho-social capacities of individual subjects.*

Ready to write

How do you feel about writing?
Fill in the table to help you focus on your attitudes.

	Always	Sometimes	Never
1 Do you feel confident about writing whenever you have to?			
2 Can you write in different styles, e.g. personal and formal letters?			
3 If you need help with your writing, are there people you can ask?			
4 Are you clear about your purpose when you write?			
5 Do you write drafts and then edit them?			
6 Do you try to avoid having to write if possible?			
7 Do you enjoy writing?			
8 Can you write to friends, family or colleagues without worrying?			
9 Do you feel confident about writing when people are watching (at work or in a post office, for example)?			
10 Do you ever write just for yourself?			
11 Is your handwriting fairly readable and quick?			

That was written by an academic who seemed to think that complex ideas have to be expressed in complex English. Otherwise no one would know how important the ideas were. Rubbish!

Simplicity is what we should be aiming at. Here is an example of simplicity which has survived a thousand years, ten thousand miles and the ordeal of translation. It comes from a poem written in AD 835 by Po Chu-i of China:

> *The world cheats those who cannot read;*
> *I, happily, have mastered script and pen.*
> *The world cheats those who hold no office;*
> *I am blessed with high official rank.*
> *Often the old have sickness and pain;*
> *With me, luckily, there is not much wrong.*

The poem uses simple words and simple images to express ideas which are grave, fundamental and universal.

Po Chu-i manages to discuss the human condition simply and coherently; the academic ties himself into a linguistic knot discussing a relatively simple idea.

Simplicity = strength!

Be yourself. Establish your own voice in what you write. Do not ape another's style.

Words and images

Close your eyes and think of England.
Let your mind play with the idea of England. What does it suggest to you?
Write down what impressions and thoughts bubbled up (if any did).

Words and images (continued)

Did your thoughts tend to be words, or were there pictures included? Here are two people's experiences:
  'Images of changing the guard at Buckingham Palace . . . soldiers marching up and down . . . the M1 motorway going from the south to the north . . .'
  'Snobbery, class, inadequate pensions, football hooliganism . . .'
  One was perhaps more full of images than the other.
  Ask other people about the way their minds work; see if they can use or like images, whether they prefer to express meanings in words, or whether they use a mixture.

Notes first

Writers who can shape a whole piece in their heads with each idea in the correct sequence are very rare indeed. Almost every great writer makes some sort of verbal 'map' before setting out into the unknown. Sometimes the map is no more than a list of key words or points. Such a list does two jobs. First, it is a reminder. It often happens when you are writing a lengthy piece that you become so interested in one aspect of the subject that you forget even to mention other equally important aspects. You may discover the lapse after the writing has been completed and then try to put matters right by forcing in an extra paragraph in the middle or tacking a new section on the end. This can be unsatisfactory because the additions upset the flow of the whole. So a list of main points before you start can be helpful. And let it be as thorough as possible. Do not delude yourself into believing that some points are so obvious you are bound to remember them without a reminder. In the excitement of writing we are all liable to forget the obvious.

But do not be too demanding of yourself if your notes are not completely comprehensive; ideas develop as you write and you usually have a chance to edit your drafts.

Another reason why notes are helpful is to establish a sequence. A shopping list is a simple reminder of what you must buy but seldom suggests the order in which you need to make your purchases. You simply tick off each item as you find it and stop shopping when everything has been bought. But a writer's list has order. It may look a bit of a jumble to an outsider, but to you it should show the bare bones of a structure, not just a heap of raw materials. You may well wish to change your plans as the real writing advances – no harm in that. But at least set out with a clear idea of your route as well as your destination. Your notes will probably incorporate not only points to be made or facts to be mentioned but also a reminder that you will need to justify certain assertions, produce evidence. The structure of a piece of writing can be very complex, yet in the hands of an expert the outcome is clear and logical. But the most complex structure is usually underpinned by an uncomplicated basic shape which has been compared with the trajectory of a golf ball: it makes a clean, strong start, passes through a high arc and then falls rapidly towards its objective, the green. During its journey it might be subject to several different forces – gravity, the weather – just as a piece of writing takes on new ideas as it proceeds. But neither the ball nor your writing should lose a sense of direction. The golfer makes his calculations before striking the ball, you should make your calculations, and put them down as notes, before beginning a piece of writing.

Make a start

The first steps at writing often seem the hardest. We are anxious to make a good start. But try not to be too fussy – make some sort of start, however lame. Perfection can come later. Get going. Keep going. Then, when you think you have said what you wanted to say, look back and study your efforts. You will almost certainly begin to see scores of things which need to be changed. Don't let it get you down – the world's greatest writers experience the very same thing.

Editing

Once you've got something down the editing process can begin.

It is a common misconception to assume that 'editing' means shortening. In fact, it can sometimes

Drafting

Try any of these to help you start. Starting is drafting.

- Jot things down as they come to mind.

- Talk into a tape recorder.

- Go somewhere where you'll feel confident about starting.

- Don't worry if you haven't got the 'right' writing materials.

- Ignore the mess and the spelling.

- Don't worry about finding the right words.

- Use shorthand for common words – you can make up your own shorthand as long as you know the meaning.

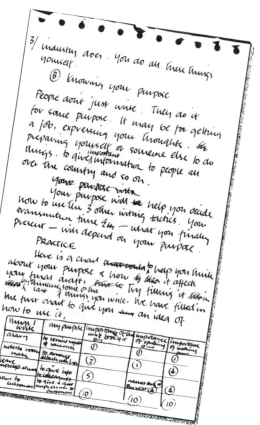

mean the very opposite. The term covers several sorts of activities, including preparing a text for printing, complete with typographical instructions. But for our purposes 'editing' activities can all be put under the broad heading of 'improving'.

When you start editing, try to identify the big problems before worrying about the little ones. Have you made your points in the right order? Is the sequence sensible or logical? Try to put yourself in the position of a stranger reading your words for the first time. Would he or she be able to understand what you are trying to convey?

Question the wisdom of your original notes. Did you set out the most sensible sequence? Try not to cling to a bad plan just because it has been around from the start. You may have to be ruthless.

The knack of being able to stand outside your own work and see it with fresh eyes is a skill that can be learned. Timing is one hint. Many writers find that their opinions of their own work vary depending on when they read it. Something which seemed brilliant just after it was completed seems dreadful a day later. Or the opposite may be true. So, take a break before re-reading what you have written. Do you still think an outsider would understand it?

Reading your work out loud to yourself is a surprisingly effective way of exposing strengths and weaknesses. It is just another way of viewing your efforts from a fresh angle.

Try asking a trusted friend for their opinion. Get some feedback. Hearing your own work adversely criticised can be as humiliating as being told you have spots. Your critic is not being cruel for the sake of it; you have asked for the comments, so listen to them.

Grammar While content and structure are the most important elements in any kind of writing, whether it is a single sentence or a whole book, spelling and grammar do matter. Serious lapses in either are bound to make a poor impression on the reader. Even the most objective judge of your work, one who is trying to find out if you know your subject, may be prejudiced by what they consider to be clumsy grammar.

Spelling Unfortunately, whereas English grammar is logical, English spelling can be a nightmare. Yet even the nightmare has logic. Some of the more common spelling mistakes can be avoided if we know the differences between such word endings as 'ent' and 'ant' and so can appreciate why 'dependant', for example, has a different sense from 'dependent'. Again, a guide to English usage should offer useful hints on the rules of spelling. Getting it right avoids ambiguity. The one comfort with written English is that it is less likely to be ambiguous than spoken English. Think of the chaos that could be caused because 'oral' and 'aural' sound the same.

A very good rule with words generally is to impose on yourself the discipline of checking with a dictionary. Check meanings of words when the context is fresh in your mind. Check spellings if in any doubt at all. But do not make these checks while you are writing the first draft of a piece.

If you keep breaking off to consult the dictionary or a grammar textbook, you may lose the flow of your writing. Bad grammar and bad spelling are more forgivable than muddled thought and jerky construction. Revise your spelling and grammar as part of the editing process.

After a while you may find yourself able to write first drafts which are quite close to a finished product. Those early efforts will have served their purpose in giving you confidence. Remember, drafts are experiments. You are not committing yourself by setting pen to paper.

You may find it useful to experiment with several different approaches to the same task before deciding which works best. Try explaining something by means of a continuous 'narrative' and then by means of sentences interspersed with numbered lists.

For example, the statement 'Most work needs time and space as well as materials and the knowledge of how to use them' can also be expressed like this:

Most work needs:

1 time

2 space

3 materials

4 knowledge

Four ways of editing

Here are four areas to look for when you edit. Try using them as guidelines.

1 Editing for meaning
When you edit for meaning you are reading to find out if your draft makes sense.

Some ways:
- Read your draft aloud and make changes in a different colour so they'll stand out.

- If you have time, leave it for a while and come back to it when your original ideas aren't so fresh in your mind.

- Leave lots of room if you write a second draft for crossing out and adding in.

2 Editing for grammar
When you edit for grammar you are checking and changing so that words and phrases are put together in the best way for your purpose.
   You are also editing for punctuation: . , : ; ' " ! ? – the signs that help the writer to communicate.

Some ways:
- Follow the suggestions given for 'Editing for meaning', but with grammar in mind.

3 Editing for spelling
Your writing purposes will help you to decide how much spelling matters. If

Which means of expressing the same notion will be the better for your purpose? It is for you to decide at the planning and editing stage.

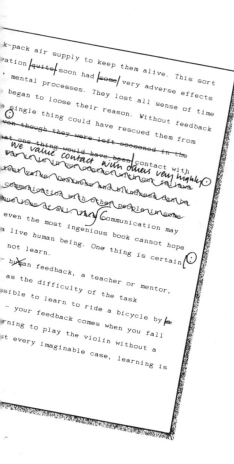

k-pack air supply to keep them alive. This sort
~ation ~~quite~~ soon had ~~some~~ very adverse effects
, mental processes. They lost all sense of time
began to loose their reason. Without feedback
~~single~~ thing could have rescued them from
~~ven though they were left cocooned in the~~
~~We value contact with others very highly~~ contact with
~~~~~~~~~~~~~~~~~~~~~~~~~~~~~
~~communication with other people in some~~
~~~~~~~~~~~~ Communication may
even the most ingenious book cannot hope
a live human being. One thing is certain
not learn.

~~hu~~man feedback, a teacher or mentor,
as the difficulty of the task
~~ss~~ible to learn to ride a bicycle by ~~~~
~ your feedback comes when you fall
~ning to play the violin without a
~t every imaginable case, learning is

your spelling is so unusual that you fail
to communicate, then you should
correct most of it. If people can still
understand what you write, perhaps it
is less important – but perhaps not.
You must decide how much spelling
matters, depending on your purpose.

Some ways:
- Underline or circle the words that
  look wrong and continue reading.
  Don't try to correct them
  immediately unless the right
  spelling comes easily.

- Decide how you are going to deal
  with misspelling – leave it? Make a
  guess? Use a dictionary? Ask
  someone?

- Get someone to look over it for
  you.

4 Editing for presentation
This means considering the overall
look, style and size: informal, large and
bold, centred on the page and so on.

Some ways:
- Know your writing purpose. Keep
  your readers clearly in mind. What
  kind of presentation would best
  communicate your message to
  them?

- Learn about the choices of
  presentation – types of layout,
  paper, handwriting, word
  processing and print.

Still worried?
A word of advice for people who after all this advice
and assurance still feel that writing is hell – try what is
called free writing. Sit down with pen and paper and

write down whatever comes into your head. Do not fret about choosing a topic. Just write. Carry on for, say, ten minutes. The result may not be the best bit of English ever written, but it may well break that block. You will discover you are able to write in a sustained way. You may be surprised to find that you have written something quite sensible. It will be a foundation which you can build on.

You should now know:
more about using notes
as a guide to writing

•

more about drafting

•

four things to look for
when editing

•

more about spelling and
grammar for different
purposes.

Last hurdles and a few surprises

If you are working towards an examination of some sort this chapter should help you considerably. If you are not, don't ignore it completely – you may well find some useful tips which you can apply to your learning.

Before the exam

Passing examinations does not depend only on how much you know, any more than it depends on luck. The vital factor is foreknowledge. You need to know what the people who set the test expect of you. By merely parading your learning, you may please yourself but you may easily fail to please the examiners.

So leave exploring the unknown to others. When you take an examination you should be sailing familiar seas. Make your studies include the nature of the examination itself, as well as the subject of the examination.

Exam requirements

Finding out the broad requirements of an examination ought to be easy but sometimes this important information can be tucked away in a college prospectus or a course syllabus. Ask questions. Try to find someone who has sat the examination before you. Keep up your inquiries until you are as confident as you can be that you have a good idea of how to satisfy the examiners' demands. Do not make assumptions. Make sure you know the facts.

Find out the form in which the examination will be set. Is it likely to include practical tests? Will there be computer-marked questionnaires? Or will it consist entirely of conventional written answers and essays? You need to know. Although the examiners will obviously guard the confidentiality of the exam paper they will almost certainly have set out the scope and nature of the questions in advance.

As you approach an examination it is worth reminding yourself of your goals. The most important aim must be to secure a pass. Naturally, you will want to put in a good paper and do the very best you can. But beware of turning pirouettes across the stage to dazzle the examiners. You could trip and tumble. Keep your sights on a pass and approach the exam in a steady, sensible way.

Exam rehearsal Part of that steady, sensible approach is rehearsing. Once you have a good grasp of what the examination is likely to contain, you can prepare yourself for a range of specific questions.

Preparing nine answers to questions which, in the event, are not set is not a waste of time if your preparation has primed you for the tenth question which really is set.

Preparing those nine answers does not mean 'swotting them up'. Rehearsing is not swotting. Rehearsing means going through the examination experience as realistically as possible.

Work

- to the time limits of the examination
- without your notes and texts
- alone
- in a quiet room
- at a time when interruptions are unlikely.

If you are studying a subject which demands physical expertise – welding, say, or cookery – then do not rely on book revision and imagination. There is no substitute for familiarity with the environment of the workshop or kitchen under examination conditions.

True, people have been known to pass written

examinations in ballroom dancing without once step-
ping on to a ballroom floor, but this is a futile exercise
offering no real skill or satisfaction.

The exam room   One extra thing about dry-run rehearsals: try to find
out about the examination room itself. We have all
noticed how an item of news means much more if we
have been to the spot where it happened. It is not just a
question of knowing the layout of the foreign town
now in the news because of street fighting. There is
something about having visited a location which
enables us in a sense to possess it. Afterwards, every
mention of the place is easier to comprehend, less
strange. It is the same with the examination room,
whether it is a hall lined with desks, a laboratory or a
workshop.

If you are fortunate, you may be taking your examination in familiar surroundings. If not, try to look at
the room well in advance. It is extraordinarily reassuring to have a picture in your mind of the examination
location while you are preparing for the event. Why be
anxious about the unknown when it is possible to find
out? After all, when the day comes you will want as
few surprises as possible.

Support   In your exam preparation you will need good feedback, support and encouragement. Ideally, this will
come from a teacher with your success at heart, but by
now you will have an established relationship through

the learning process with one or more trusted mentors. They should have the sensitivity not to overburden you with quibbles about your performance in the run-up to the examination. Let whoever is your source of feedback point you firmly at certain mistakes you can cope with. If something has gone awry in your studies you need to be able to take specific action to put matters right.

Revision   One of the most important advantages of understanding in advance the nature of the examination is that it helps you revise. Level-headed people can become quite irrational about revision. They compulsively re-read everything they have ever read in their studies, plough through their notes trying to commit every word to memory. It would almost be better if they did no revision at all. For revision without method can clog your thoughts and impair your frame of mind. It does nothing for clarity and ready recall.

The first step is to find out how much revision you should do. It varies from person to person and subject to subject. Ask your course tutor or anyone competent to give guidance. It should be someone who knows you and who knows the course and the examination.

Next, using all the guidance you can get, set out a feasible programme of revision over a period of weeks. Allot specific tasks to specific periods. Write these down in a diary or as a wall chart.

How about using the same sort of timetable as in Chapter 3?

Change the time divisions to suit your day.

Your notes   This is when the notes you have been taking throughout your course should be coming into their own. These notes will not only contain revision information but will act as keys to unlock your memory. Just as a theatre prompter does not need to recite a whole speech to jog an actor's memory, so your notes will probably trigger whole segments of your studies with a few words. This may not work for you, but that does not mean you have to embark on a massive re-reading programme. Skimming a text is a perfectly acceptable trick. You will be surprised how your head will home in on the passages it needs to know for examination purposes. You have been trusting your own ability all along, don't stop now.

Your state of mind

Before and during an exam your state of mind may prove crucial. How do you feel about exams? Have a go at the quiz below, *How anxious are you?*

How anxious are you?

Put a tick by your answer to each question. (See p. 136 for comments.)

Some people get very nervous about taking tests or exams. Which of these statements is nearest to your attitude?
- I don't understand why they worry so much – there's nothing to fear.
- ✗ I understand, but don't suffer myself.
- I get fairly nervous at the thought myself. ✓
- I am one of them!

If you do well in one test or exam paper, what effect does that have on your performance?
- It boosts my confidence in future tests.
- ✗ It makes me feel a bit more confident. ✓
- It makes me worried in case I can't do as well all the time.
- It makes no difference at all.

In general, how do you feel about tests and exams?
- They are great, and I'm good at them.
- They are useful in a limited way. ✓
- They are unreliable and unnecessary.
- ✗ They are much too stressful; I would do better if they didn't exist.

Before taking a test or exam, how do you feel?
- Extremely nervous about it.
- I have a terrific need to cram right up to the last minute.
- ✗ A bit tense but I try to relax the night before. ✓
- Fine.

How do you perform during the test or exam?
- I get so nervous that I freeze completely.
- ✗ Because of nerves I forget things that I really know.
- My nerves tend to steady once I get going. ✓
- My feelings have no effect at all on my performance.

During tests and exams do you find yourself getting at all distracted?
- I worry all the time because I think

Mood management is something we all try to master from childhood onwards; despite our efforts we remain at the mercy of our moods. We find ourselves swinging from glee to gloom in a matter of moments and often for the silliest reasons. What is worse, our attempts at mood-changing sometimes make matters worse. This is very true of examinations.

If we manipulate ourselves into a state of great confidence before an examination, we may lose that vital

other people are doing better than me.

- I keep thinking about what marks I'm going to get, and that puts me off. ✓
- I sometimes find myself getting distracted but I can pull myself together and get on with it.
- No, I shut out everything but the questions.

After the test or exam is over, how do you feel about it?
- I feel so tense that my stomach gets upset.
- I try to stop worrying about my performance, but I can't.
- I often think I could have done better than I did.
- I take the view that what's done is done and hope for the best. ✓

During a test or exam what would you do if you thought you were getting behind or going badly wrong?
- It would fill me with despair – I would feel like giving up.
- I would struggle through to the end somehow. ✓
- I would try to finish at least one thing properly.
- I would take stock and work out the best way to use the rest of my time.

How do you organise the weeks before the test or exam?
- I go through everything from start to finish without any plan.
- I try to cover things I have missed out.
- I have a revision plan in which I try to work through everything systematically.
- I have a revision plan which focuses on exactly what the exam requires, and nothing more. ✓

How much practice in test or exam conditions do you have?
- A lot – at least four sessions or more.
- Some – two or three sessions. ✓
- Just one session.
- None.

How anxious are you?

There are no right and wrong answers to these questions – they are meant to help you find out (if you didn't already know) how you feel about the potential anxieties of exams. Bear in mind your answers as you read the rest of this chapter.

spark of anxiety which fires our imagination or power to organise our thoughts. Actors declare that unless they are nervous before going on stage their performances are mediocre. They forget their lines or lose their grip on characterisation. On the other hand, extreme nervousness can be crippling. Sickness, sleeplessness and stomach cramps never helped anyone to give their best.

What we need to achieve is a state of mind somewhere between over-assurance and acute anxiety. This much is obvious, but getting there is harder. At the start of this book we spoke of the conflicting voices in our heads. Pay too much attention to that Devil Who Says Don't and we will end up with a dull life, and the epitaph 'He never took a chance', 'She always played safe'. Take too much notice of that ambitious voice spurring us on to ridiculous goals and we will end up with nothing but a broken spirit.

The same voices will be talking to you in the run-up to the examination. Although they are in conflict, they have the same intention – your happiness. They just have very different ways of going about it. The voice that says 'Panic!' is in its way being protective. It is preparing you for a possible emergency. The voice that says 'There's nothing to worry about' believes that preserving your self-esteem and equanimity, even in the very short term, is supremely important.

Letting either voice score a total victory is potentially disastrous. Our true self-interest lies somewhere in the middle where we have a third voice struggling to keep a sense of proportion.

Anxiety   You probably agree that extreme nervousness afflicts more examination candidates than extreme complacency. So how can you ease that nervousness?

If your feelings are in a turmoil in the days and hours before the test, ask yourself a few blunt questions:

- If I failed would I be doomed to live the rest of my life in despair?

- Would failure prove I am an irredeemable idiot?

- Would I never have another chance to succeed?

- Is this my only opportunity to break through into a richer enjoyment of leisure or career?

To answer 'yes' to any of these questions would be preposterous. Life never closes the door. Exams can be taken again. To start thinking in over-dramatic terms is daft and self-destructive. By completing the studies that have brought you to the examination room, you have already demonstrated to the world, if not to your doubting self, that you are a person to be reckoned with. You have already achieved some stature in the eyes of others by your tenacity of purpose, together with all you have learned from life before your studies began.

Now have the sense to see that stature yourself. If you were incapable of success, you would never have reached the examination room. Remind yourself of your reasons, your goals. Return to that glimpse of the future, the light at the end of the tunnel when your studies become tedious. The light still shines, and it is much closer now.

One sure way to renew your sense of proportion is to talk to someone else. Ask your mentor. As we discovered in earlier chapters, this useful soul need not be an expert on your subject but merely a sensible friend who is prepared to be patient, listen and respond constructively.

In or out of the family, in or out of the classroom, such a mentor can be particularly valuable before an examination. Anxiety feeds on itself and grows into a monster if you allow your thoughts to turn round and round in your head.

A quiet chat with a mentor makes you realise that

you allowed yourself to get into a flap unnecessarily. Pick your mentor wisely (not necessarily for brilliance, but rather for level-headed sense) and you will have found a friend indeed.

Over-confidence The trouble with over-confidence is that it is a little like drunkenness: the condition itself impairs your ability to recognise it. Check your 'sobriety' by conversation with friends. A wise mentor may firmly put your feet back on the ground by reminding you of that gloomy old saying: 'Pride comes before a fall.' If you feel supremely sure of yourself it may be a particular sort of self-delusion designed to protect you from unhappiness. This is a discouraging thought but there is often a lot of truth in it.

Assessment and self-assessment

The examination is an extreme example of the assessment of an individual's ability. Assessment is the process of quantifying knowledge, reasoning, or ability. Evaluation is the word used for more long-term, less objective judgement. We are chiefly concerned with assessment, not only of the examination variety but of the self-examination kind, too.

Objective self-assessment is a great skill but easier than the imponderables of self-evaluation. If you are an employer considering engaging someone as a typist, it is relatively easy to assess typing skills for speed and accuracy, but much more difficult to evaluate whether the typist's temperament would fit in with other employees. It follows that in self-assessment you need to establish benchmarks of performance.

Set yourself timed tasks, ranging over hours, days and months. Be ready to change your self-imposed requirements if they prove unrealistic or unreasonable, but all the while monitor your progress. This way you will prevent yourself drifting uncertainly, not knowing how well or badly you are faring. Once again, do not go it alone with your self-assessment. Get constructive feedback from teachers and the blessing of friends prepared to share the journey with you – your mentors.

A swimmer can judge time and distance without outside help, but needs someone at the poolside to assess style. That someone is the swimmer's mentor. When it comes to the much broader judgement of evaluation, the swimmer still needs a mentor but must answer self-imposed questions such as:

- Is it worth it?

- What have I gained by my efforts?

- Have I won what I wanted?

The eve of an examination is no time for this sort of inner question. Trust the judgement you reached when first embarking on your studies and setting your goals. Confine your self-questioning to assessing your progress towards examination success.

Earlier we offered the example of the taxi driver paralysed in an accident who, left with no physical power except speech, remembered an old ambition – yodelling. She studied and became a successful entertainer.

At every stage it was possible to assess her progress and even now, when she tours the pubs with her yodelling act, she can grade her success by means of the money and applause she earns. But whether, upon stringent evaluation, she has got what she wanted we can scarcely say. Contentment, self-fulfilment, these are elusive qualities not easy to measure.

Either in assessment or in evaluation it can be a big mistake to take other people's performances as our own yardstick. If we judge ourselves exclusively by what someone else has done, we forget that our declared intention is to reach the goal we set ourselves at the start.

Exams

When it comes to an exam paper you will probably not have time for a first draft. Anyway, by then you'll be able to cope without one. Just make a few brief notes to remind yourself of what information and ideas you want to express, and in what order.

And remember: simplicity = strength. If you do not

know the answer to the question, you will not fool the examiner by putting up a smoke-screen of empty jargon and complex sentence structures.

Bear in mind that appearances matter, too. The way your work is presented should be designed to help the reader understand your words. When making your notes you will already have decided on a sensible sequence. Now add to the logic of your construction by the use of paragraphs and headings.

Paragraphs should not be used arbitrarily to break up long slabs of sentences. They should be used as a sign that a new topic or a new aspect of the same topic has been reached.

There are no firm rules for the use of paragraphs but the guiding principle in this as in everything else to do with writing is your purpose and the meaning you want to convey. Is it easily understandable? Would it be better understood if expressed another way?

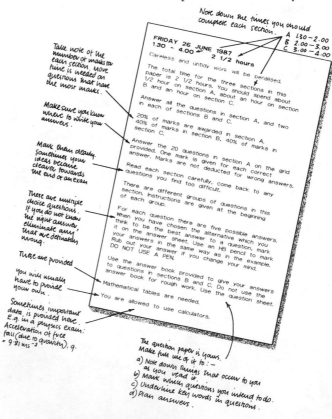

Exam tips

Key words explained – these instructions are often given in exam questions, especially essays:

Compare:	Are the things very alike (similar) or are there important differences? Which do you think is best? Why?
Contrast:	Look for differences.
Criticise:	Use evidence to support your opinion on the value or merit of theories, facts or views of others.
Define:	Give the meaning.
Describe:	Write in detail.
Differentiate:	Explain the difference.
Discuss:	Write about the important aspects of the topic. Are there two sides to the question? Consider the arguments for and against.
Distinguish:	Explain the difference.
Evaluate:	Judge the importance or success.
Explain:	Make clear.
Illustrate:	Give examples which make the point clear.
Interpret:	Explain the meaning in your own words; for example, you may be asked to interpret a graph.
Justify:	Give reasons to support an argument or action.
Outline:	Choose the most important aspects of a topic. Ignore the minor detail.
Relate:	Show the connection between things.
State:	Write briefly the main point.
Summarise:	Bring together the main points.
Trace:	Show how something has developed from beginning to end.

Key stages in answering exam questions:
1　Scan all questions.
2　Mark all the questions you could answer.
3　Read these questions carefully.
4　Choose the correct number (in each section).
5　Decide on an order: best answers first.
6　Divide up your time.
7　Underline key words in the question.
8　Plan your answer. Stick to the point of the question.
9　Write your answer. Use the plan at every stage, e.g. paragraph by paragraph.
10　Check your answer against the plan. Look out for mistakes.

During the exam

Have a go at *Ten instructions* overleaf. You may learn something from it!

Ask away　　Remember when taking practical tests that you are allowed to ask questions as well as answer them. The

141

Ten instructions

Follow the instructions numbered 1–10.

1 Pick up a pen.
2 Sign your name.
3 Put the pen down again.
4 Do a couple of sit-ups.
5 Open a window.
6 Take a few deep breaths.
7 Close the window.
8 Sit down.
9 Cross your legs.
10 Ignore instructions 1–9.

These instructions hold a lesson for all examination candidates.

Did you do 1–9 before seeing 10? This is an old trick which fools many people. What would you say the moral of the exercise is? Read carefully and fully before you act? YES! Make sure you really understand the question before you start scribbling your answer or plunge into a practical test.

questions in a written test are supposed to be complete and unambiguous. If you find an ambiguity, then consider saying so cautiously in your answer. But if you are uncertain how to proceed with a practical test then seek clarification. Are you allowed to use a calculator? Ask the invigilator. There is no sense in blundering on when asking a question will clear things up. The worst that can happen is that the invigilator will decline to give guidance. You will have lost nothing by asking.

When something goes wrong A common source of anxiety during examinations is the discovery of an error in figure work. The candidate has been working on a mathematical calculation, for

example, but it comes out wrongly. If the fault lies in a slip which exists throughout the calculation, all is not lost. As long as the calculation itself has followed the right lines, your answer is not totally invalid. The examiner is not looking for ways to fail you.

On the contrary, the examiner is seeking signs that you know what you are doing. A silly slip does not indicate that you are ignorant. So when your calculation refuses to resolve itself correctly although your method has been sound, write a note to the examiner as part of your answer, recognising your error, identifying the point at which you went wrong, but defending your approach to the problem.

It will then still be open to the examiner to give you marks at least high enough for a pass.

Answer the question   To get what you want, give the examiner what the examiner wants. That is the great secret. No less and no more. Do not parade the depth and width of your learning. Do not answer questions that have not been asked. All that will come of such a display is an increased risk of making mistakes. So do not give a firework display when you have been asked only to strike a match. Remember – answer the question, the whole question, and nothing but the question.

Ignoring others   Whatever happens, do not be deflated by what you see other candidates doing. If the person at the next desk is writing furiously while you are still sitting there, weighing up the question, take no notice. Trust your own judgement. Do not be bounced into untimely activity. Do not assume that the fastest and most voluminous writer in the room is the best student. It is not a race. You are competing for nothing except the understanding and approval of the examiner. Your sole aim is to pass. What happens to anyone else in the room is of minimal concern beyond the natural ties of friendship.

You should now
know more about how
to rehearse for an exam

●

be clearer about how to
revise

●

know more about what
to do in the exam.

Things to remember

Although there have been a good number of specific hints about how to organise your studies, the dominant theme has been one of attitudes. It is the personal philosophy behind your work which is important. And at the heart of all our advice on attitudes lies a two-word message: trust yourself.

You are already adept at learning.

You already have a good command of language.

Establish not only your goal but the reasons for it. It may be that you want simply to be able to earn more money or have more fun. Or it may be something much less pragmatic, such as the desire to escape your present circumstances or become what you conceive to be a more educated person.

Tell yourself the truth about your own motives. Lay down your aims and get to work, not with pig-headed refusal to change in the light of experience, but with sensible determination. Trust yourself, for you are your own boss. You are no longer a child to be intimidated. You are a student in control of your own learning. You are a customer; the course and those who conduct it are there to help you, indeed to serve you. Treat them with civility but remember that it is up to you to be in charge. Be demanding. Do not be fobbed off.

And here is one abundantly encouraging thought to end with.

When you set out on a course of learning, however modest the subject, you never really know where it will lead. You make your plans, set your sights. But the world is wonderfully unpredictable, full of surprises.

By opening your mind to knowledge you are inviting life to touch you in new ways. The human mind needs other minds to feed it. Fed this way, your mind will quite probably go off on excursions you never imagined possible at the start.

A life that once seemed stimulating can look quite humdrum in retrospect when learning has opened new horizons.

Further information

How to find the course you want

In the Know is about learning skills that you
once you have started your course or progra
study. But what about getting on a course in t
place? What courses are there in your area? H(
you choose between them? Here are some or,
sations which may be able to help you.

Libraries Your local library should be able to give you inform
tion on local education opportunities. Ask at th
information desk of the reference section.

Citizens' Advice Bureau Your nearest Citizens' Advice Bureau will also give
you information. They should be able to guide you on
financial entitlements for study too.

The Careers Service The Careers Service is run by the Local Education
Authority and mainly provides advice for school and
college leavers, but some services also give advice to
people of all ages.

Job Centres Ask at your local Job Centre for information on local
training opportunities, including Manpower Services
Commission (MSC) courses.

Education Guidance Services There is a network of local services throughout the UK
providing information on education and training for
adults in their area. A free directory of these services is
available from: ECCTIS, PO Box 88, Walton Hall,
Milton Keynes MK7 6DB. Tel: 0908 368921, or look
in *Second Chances* (see Booklist).

National Advisory Centre on Careers for Women

This centre offers advice to women on suitable careers. More information is available from: National Advisory Centre on Careers for Women, Drayton House, 30 Gordon Street, London WC1H 0AX. Tel: 01-380 0117.

National Institute of Adult Continuing Education (NIACE)

A national body which has a good information service; its library is open to anyone. More information is available from: NIACE, 19b De Montfort Street, Leicester LE1 7GE. Tel: 0553 5514512.

Scottish Institute of Adult Education (SIAE)

An information centre for adult education in Scotland. More information is available from: SIAE, 30 Rutland Square, Edinburgh EH1 2BW. Tel: 031-229 0331 or 229 0311.

Training Access Points (TAP)

This is a new computerised service from the MSC. It aims to improve public access to information and advice on training and education opportunities related to employment. The TAP service has information at local and national level and is based in places such as public libraries and Job Centres. Ask at either place if there is a TAP in your area.

Higher Education Information Service (HEIS)

The HEIS gives information about course opportunities in professional and higher education throughout the UK. Full details are available from: HEIS, Middlesex Polytechnic, 114 Chase Side, London N14 5PN. Tel: 01-886 6599.

For more detailed information on the opportunities open to you, have a look at *Second Chances* (see Booklist). It includes advice particularly for women, the disabled, the elderly, ethnic minorities, the unemployed and people with children.

Money

There's no getting away from it – studying costs money. If you want to study in the evenings, for example, you'll need money for books and equipment; if you're studying away from home you will need money to live on.

And then there's the course fees. Whereas many

further education or vocational training schemes are cheap or free, some higher education is not. If you start a full-time degree course you will automatically get a (mandatory) grant. Unfortunately this does not always apply to part-time and Open University courses. Grants for these courses do exist (discretionary), but are hard to come by. Nevertheless financial help may well be available, so for more information contact: Department of Education and Science, Room 4/50, Elizabeth House, York Road, London SE1 7PH; Scottish Education Department Awards Branch, Haymarket House, Clifton Terrace, Edinburgh EH12 5DT; Department of Education for Northern Ireland, Rathgael House, Balloo Road, Bangor, County Down BT19 2PR.

More information on the financial aspects of studying is given in *Second Chances* edited by Pates and Good (see Booklist).

Booklist

ANSELL, GWEN *Make the most of your memory* National Extension College, 1985.

BADDELEY, ALAN *Your memory: a user's guide* Penguin, new edn, pbk, 1983.

BUZAN, TONY *Use your head* BBC Books, 2nd rev. edn, 1984.

DAVIES, DON *Maximising examination performance: a psychological approach* Kogan Page, 1986.

DE BONO, EDWARD *Teaching thinking* Penguin, new edn, pbk, 1979.

DOWNS, SYLVIA *How do I learn?* Longman, 1985.

FREEMAN, R. *Mastering study skills* Macmillan, 1982.

GOOD, MARTIN *Write on* ALBSU, 1986.

HOUSTON, JOHN P. *Fundamentals of learning and memory* Academic Press, 2nd rev. edn, 1986.

Improve your learning Longman/COIC, 1983.

Improve your reading Longman/COIC, 1986.

Improve your writing Longman/COIC, 1984.

INGLIS, J. and LEWIS, R. *Clear thinking* National Extension College, 1980.

LEWIS, R. *How to write essays* National Extension College, 1976; Heinemann, rev. edn, pbk, 1979.

PATES, A. and GOOD, M. (eds) *Second chances: the guide to adult education and training opportunities* COIC, 6th edn, 1987.

SCOTT, JOHN and ROCHESTER, ARTHUR *Effective management skills: managing people* Sphere, 1987.

SHONE, RONALD *Creative visualisation: how to use imagery and imagination for self-improvement* Thorsons, 1984.

SULLIVAN, TONY *Studying* National Extension College (Studying Skills series), 1978.

Index

Acknowledgements

The following extracts are copyright and have been reproduced in this book with the permission of the copyright-holders concerned:

Extracts from *The effective learner* by Martin Good, Cambridge Training and Development Ltd (The Open College, 1987):

page
14	'Early learning'
23	'What motivates you?'
25	'Your needs'
31–2	'Getting the message'
37	'Could you tell me – ?'
53	'How organised are you?'
68–9	'Advice on priorities'
91	'Be prepared'
112–13	'Advantages, risks, issues'
120–1	'Words and images'
134–5	'How anxious are you?'

Extracts from *How to study and pass exams* by M. Coles and C. White (Collins Educational, 1982):

page
58	'Progress report'
81	Library coding diagram
93	'Skimming the cream'
94	'Scanning the page'
96	'Select/reject'
97	'Reading strategies'
98	'Comparing notes'
99	'Key words'
101	'Sprays'
102	'In short'
140	Exam paper illustration
141	'Exam tips'

Extracts from *Improve your writing* by Martin Good (Longman/COIC, 1984):

page
119   'Ready to write'
123   'Drafting'
126–7   'Four ways of editing'

Extracts from *Time management made easy* by Peter Turla and Kathleen L. Hawkins (Grafton Books, a division of the Collins Publishing Group, 1985):

page
54–5   'Your time'
59   'Am I interrupting myself?'
66   'Priority grid'
67   'A few tips'
68   'The 4 Ds'

Extracts from *Finding out* (COIC, 1985). The material is Crown copyright, and is reproduced with the permission of Her Majesty's Stationery Office:

page
74–5   'Finding out'
75   'Your access skills'
77   'Library quiz'

Extract from *Chinese poems* translated by Arthur Waley (Allen & Unwin, 1982):

page
120   part of 'A mad poem addressed to my
        nephews and nieces' by Po Chu-i

The following extracts are based on activities in a life and career planning course run by Maurice Bailey and Dick Saxton:

page
23   'Setting objectives'
65   'Ten things I want to do in my life'

From *Second chances: the guide to adult education and training opportunities* edited by Andrew Pates and Martin Good (COIC, 1987):

page
89   boxed extracts

The following are based on an unpublished book on achievement motivation in study by Tim Eiloart; thanks also to *Teaching achievement motivation* by A. Alchular, D. Tabor and J. McIntyre, Education Ventures Inc, Hartford, Connecticut, USA:

page
25–8   'The nAch quiz'
46–50   'Your learning personality'

Notes